YOUR CAT IS TRYING TO

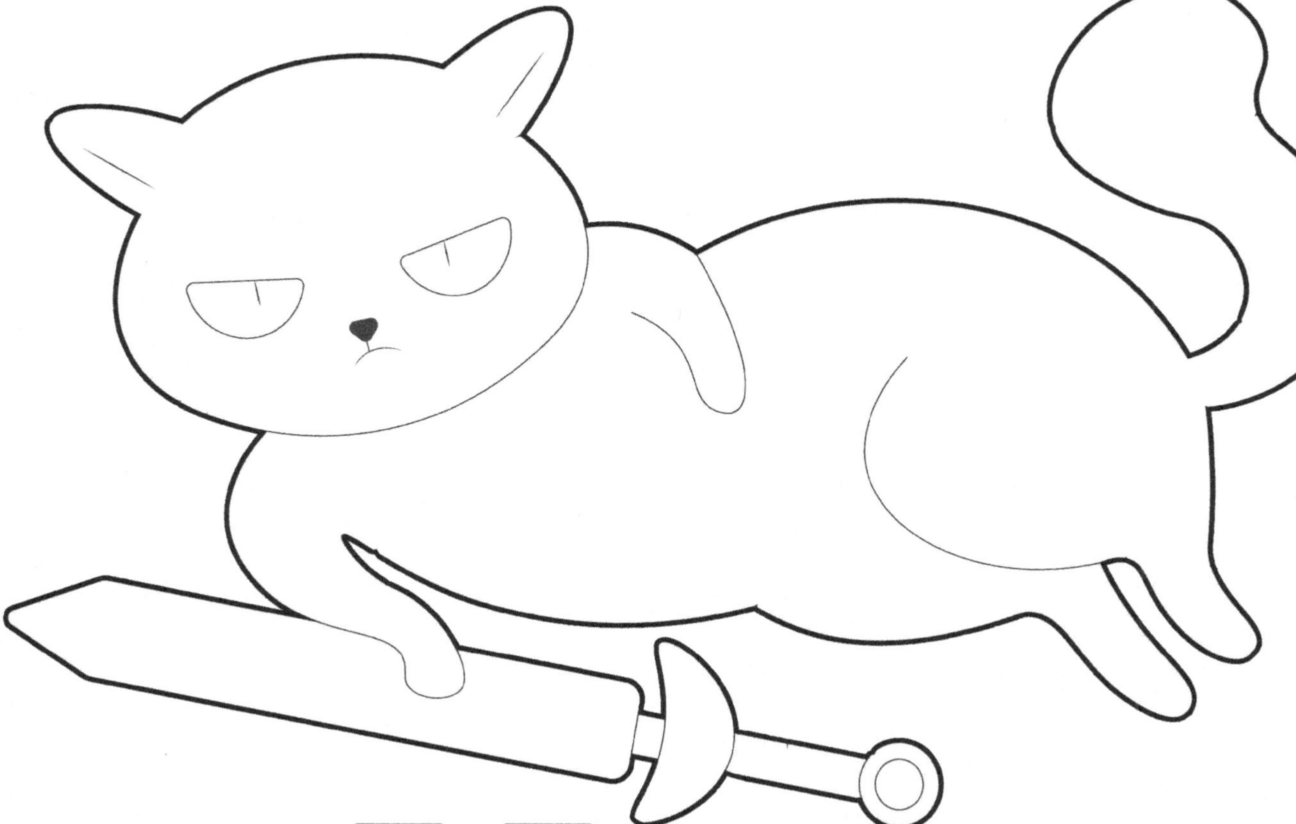

KILL YOU

STRAIGHT OUTTA COLOR

StraightOuttaColor.com

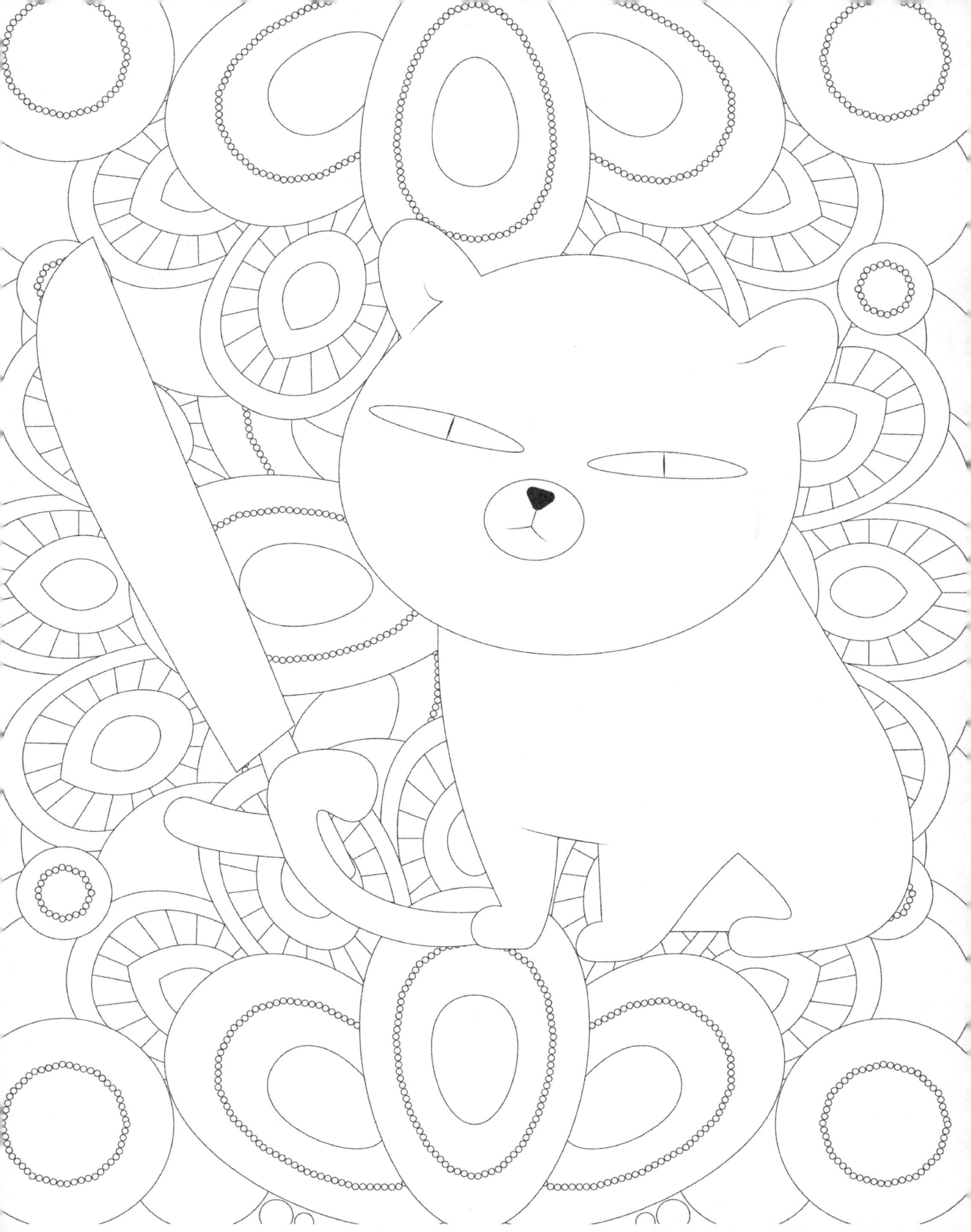

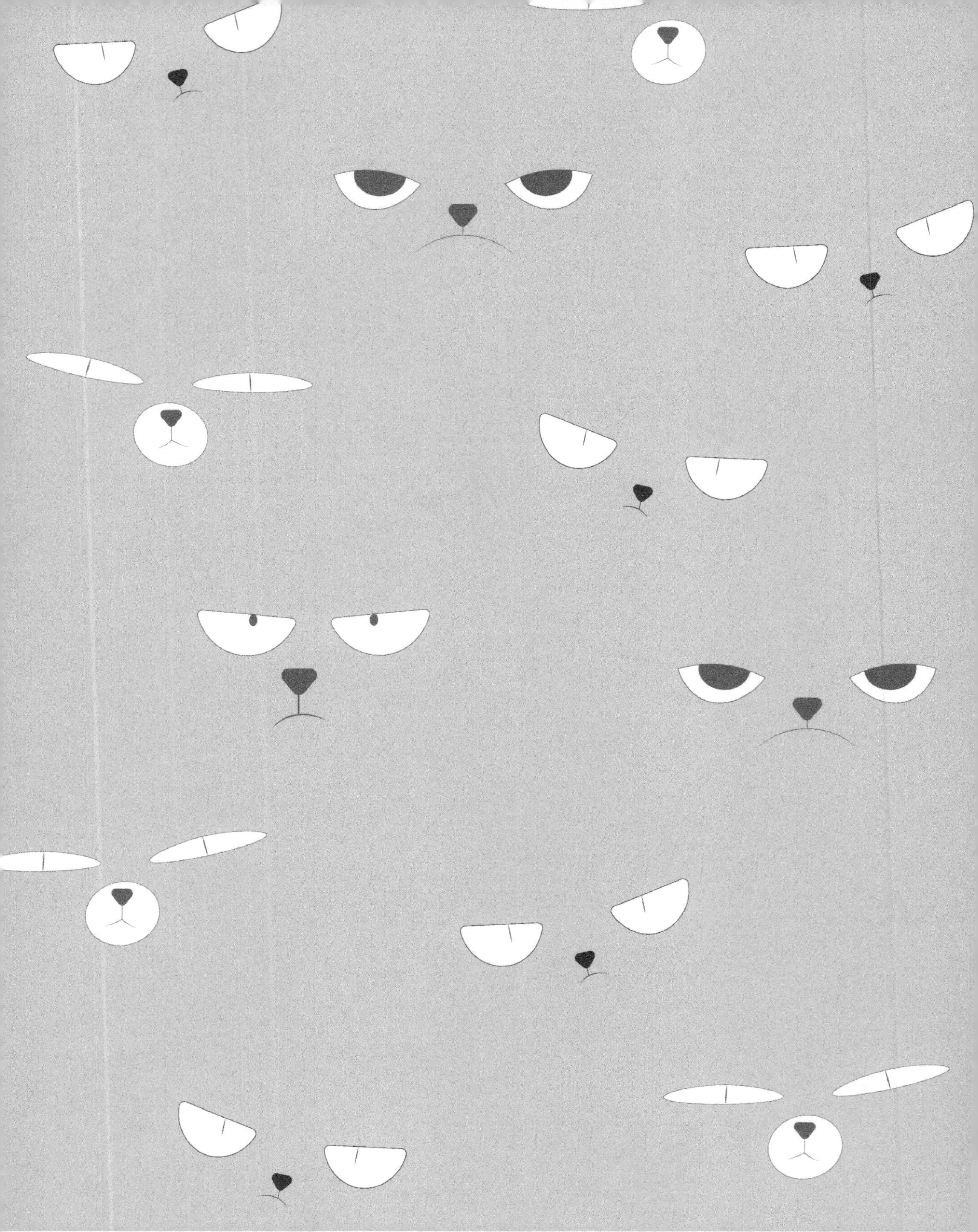

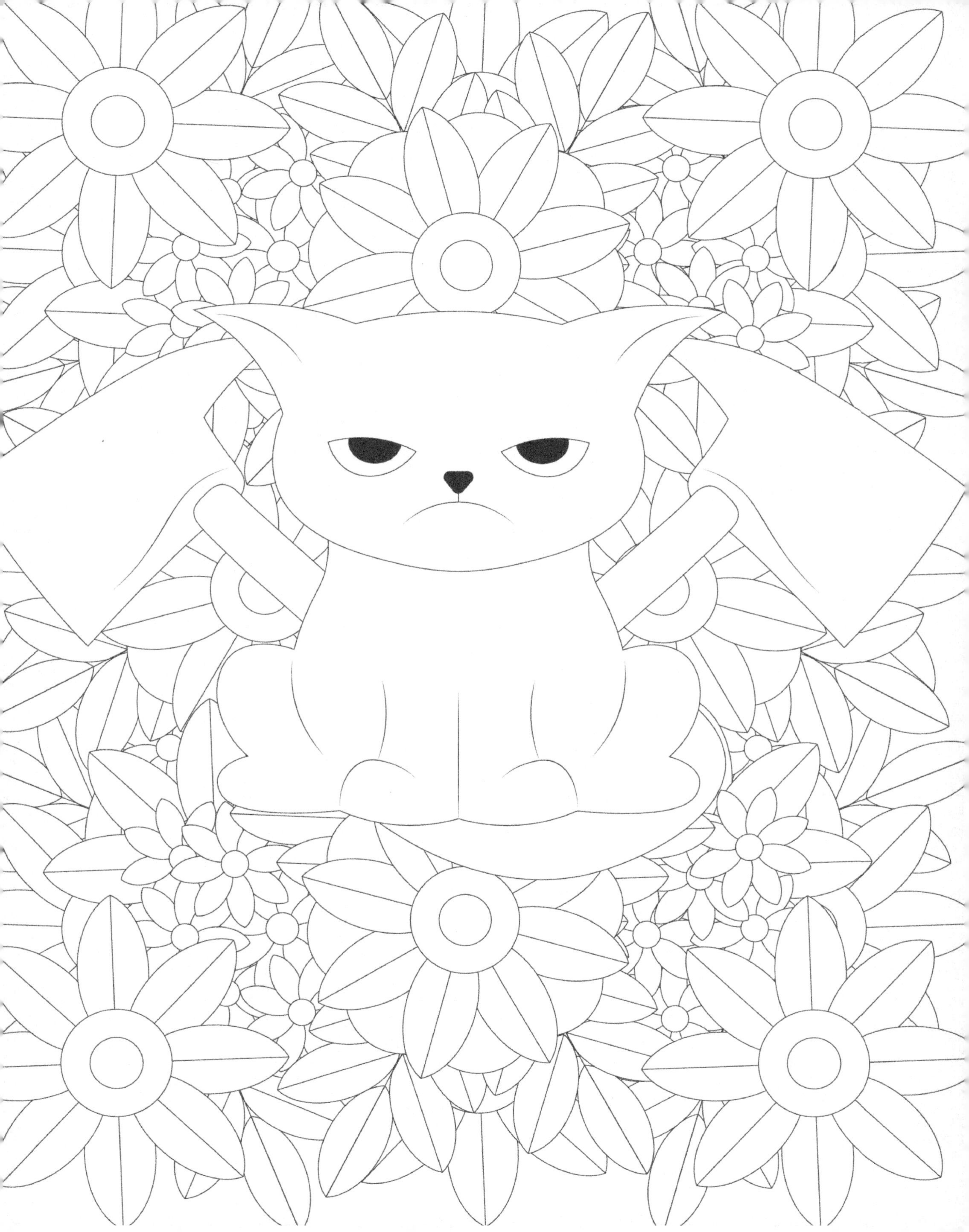

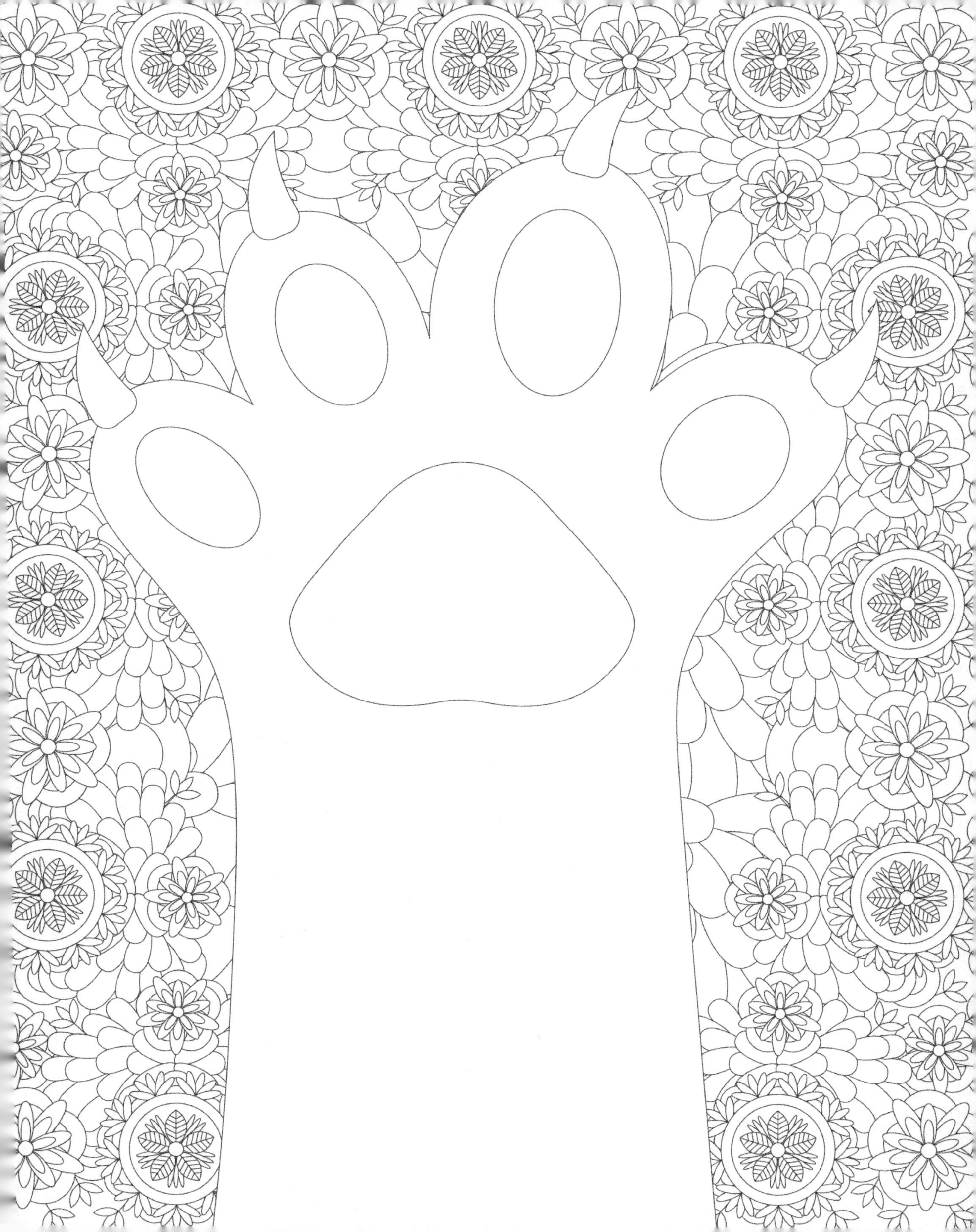

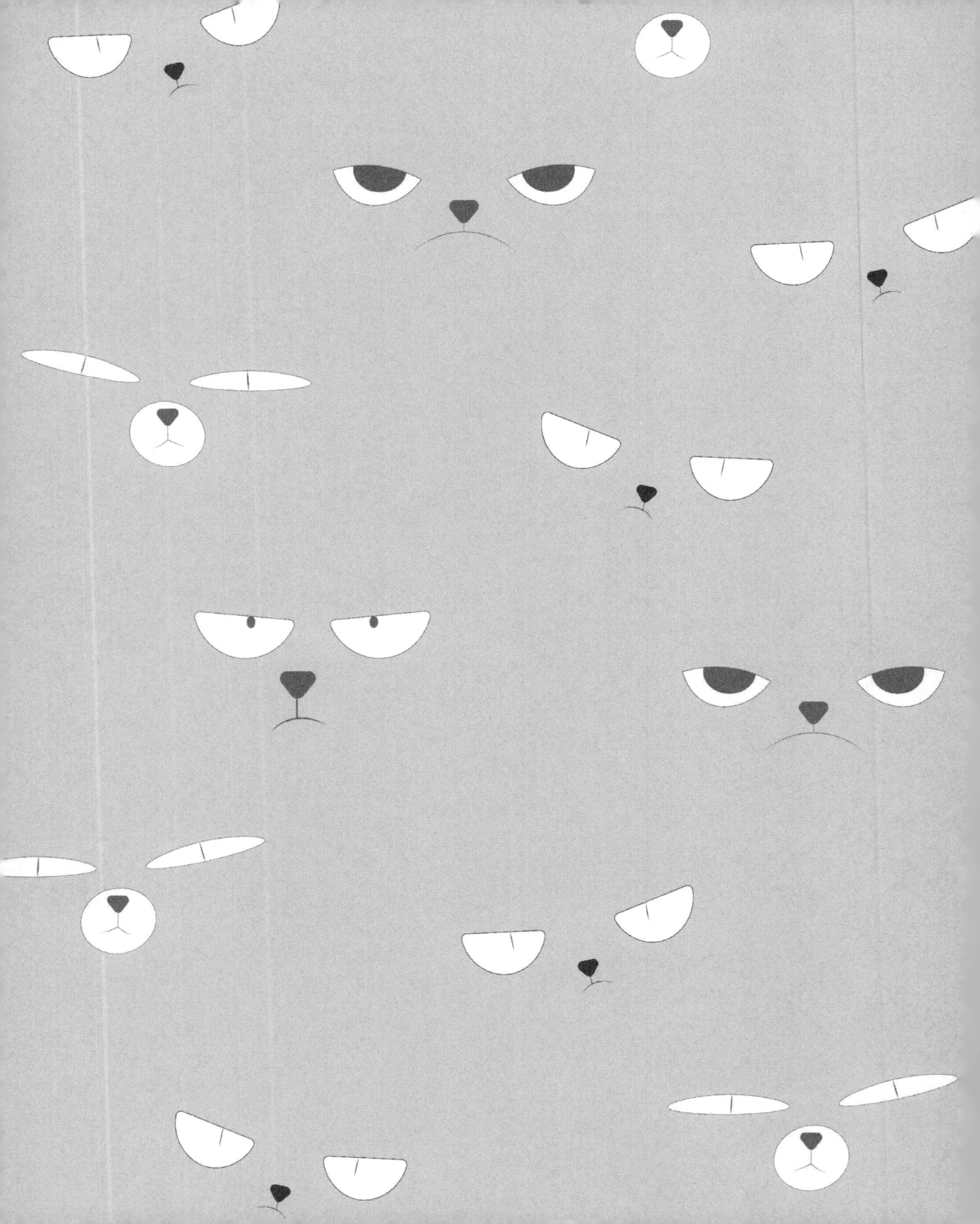

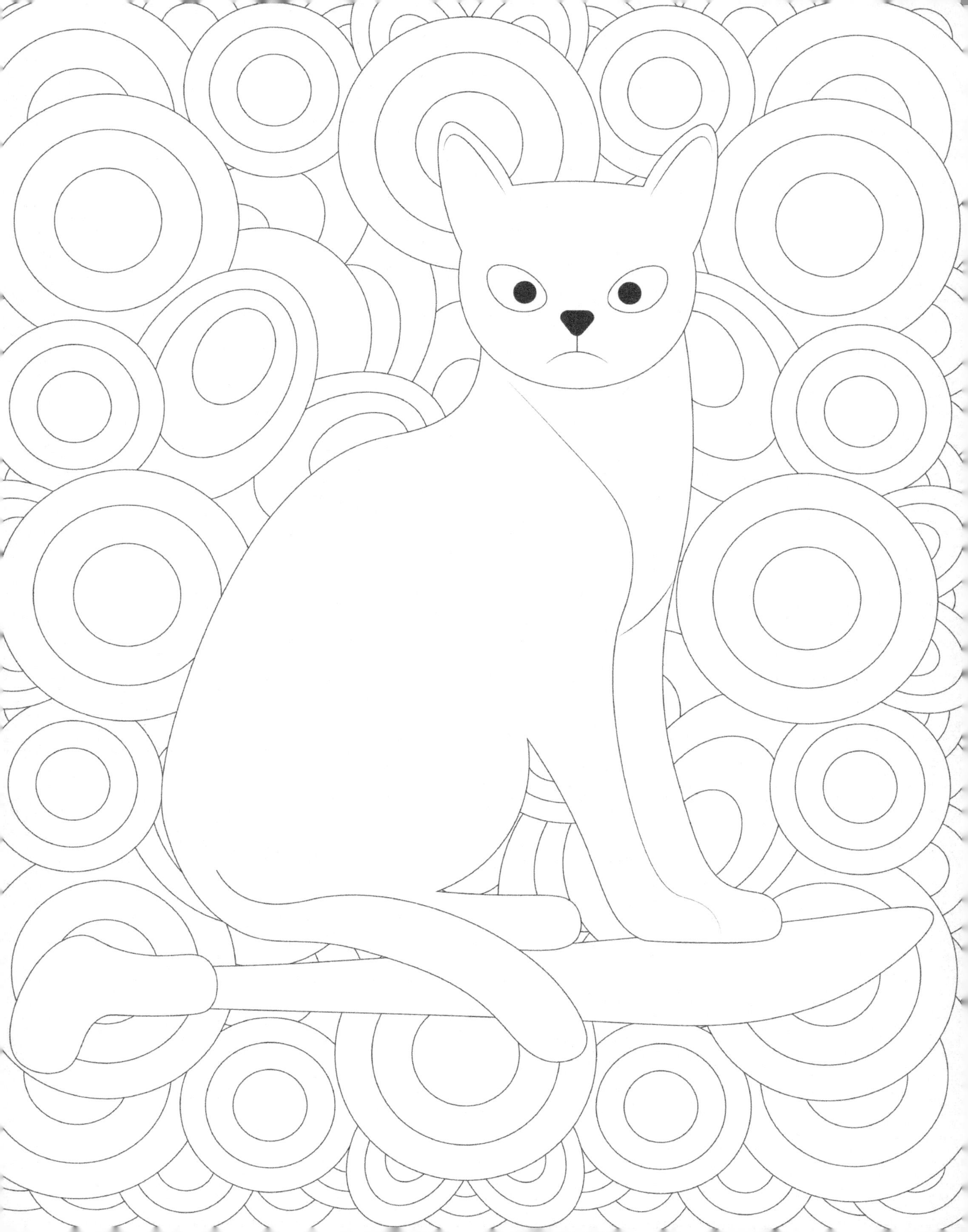

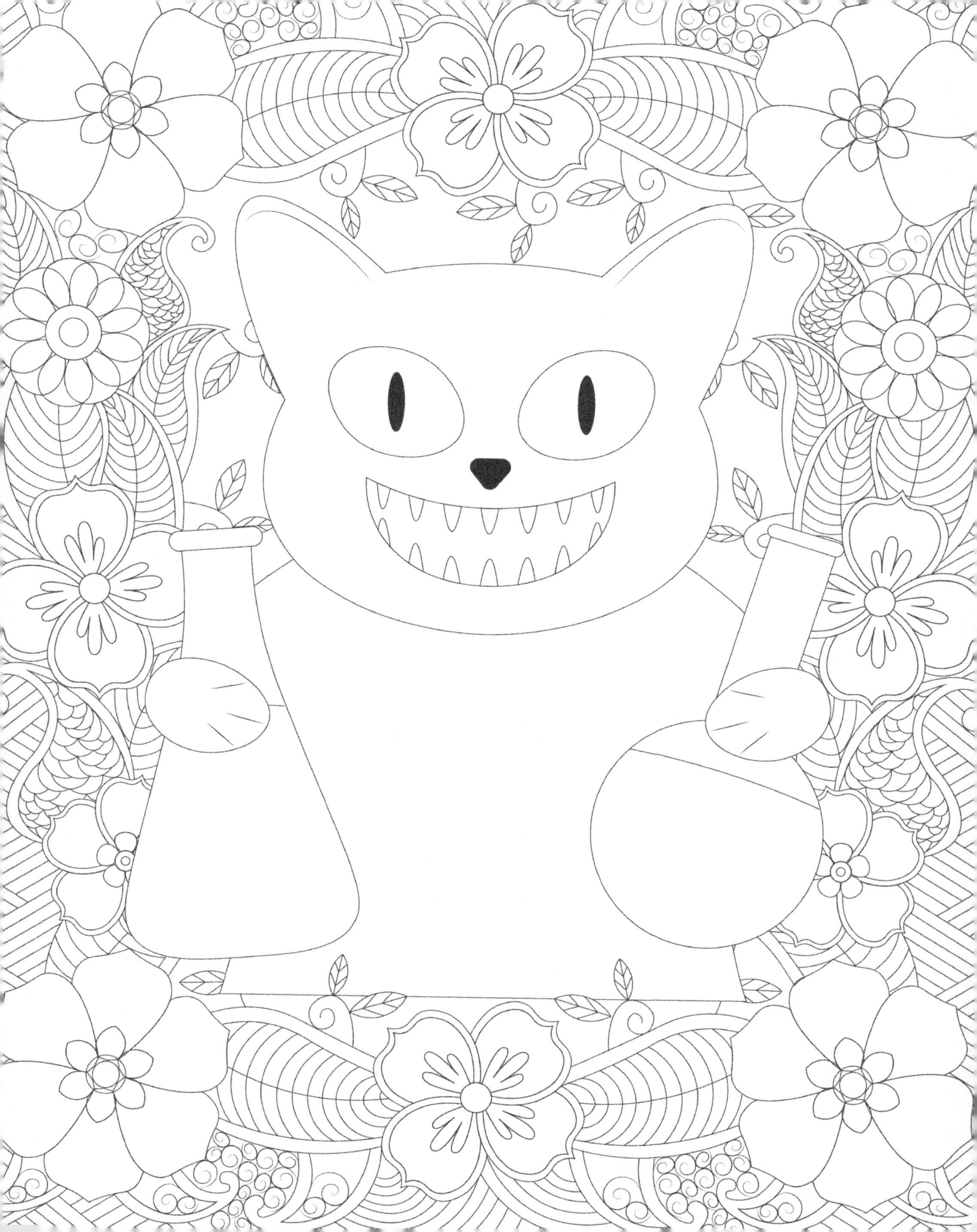

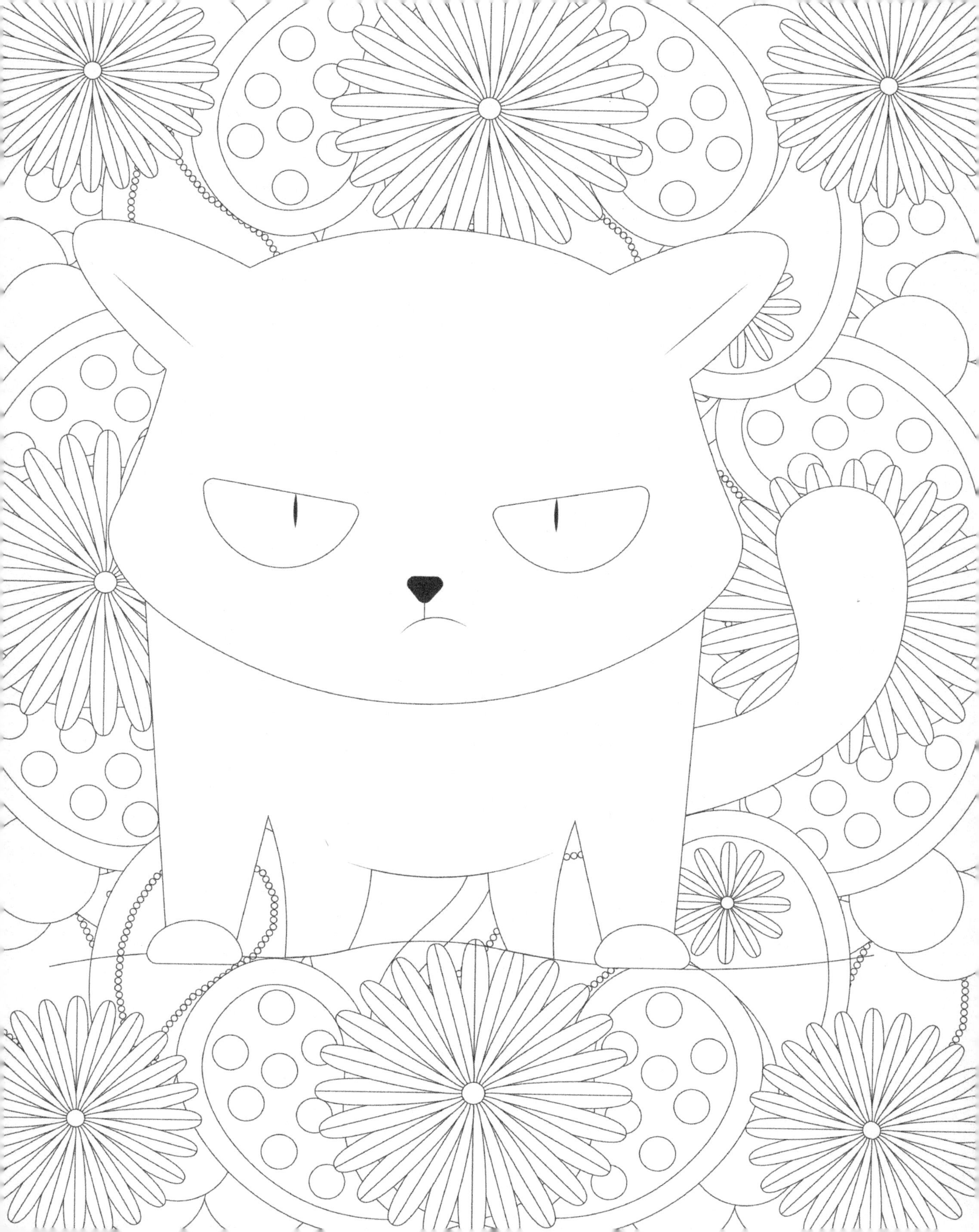

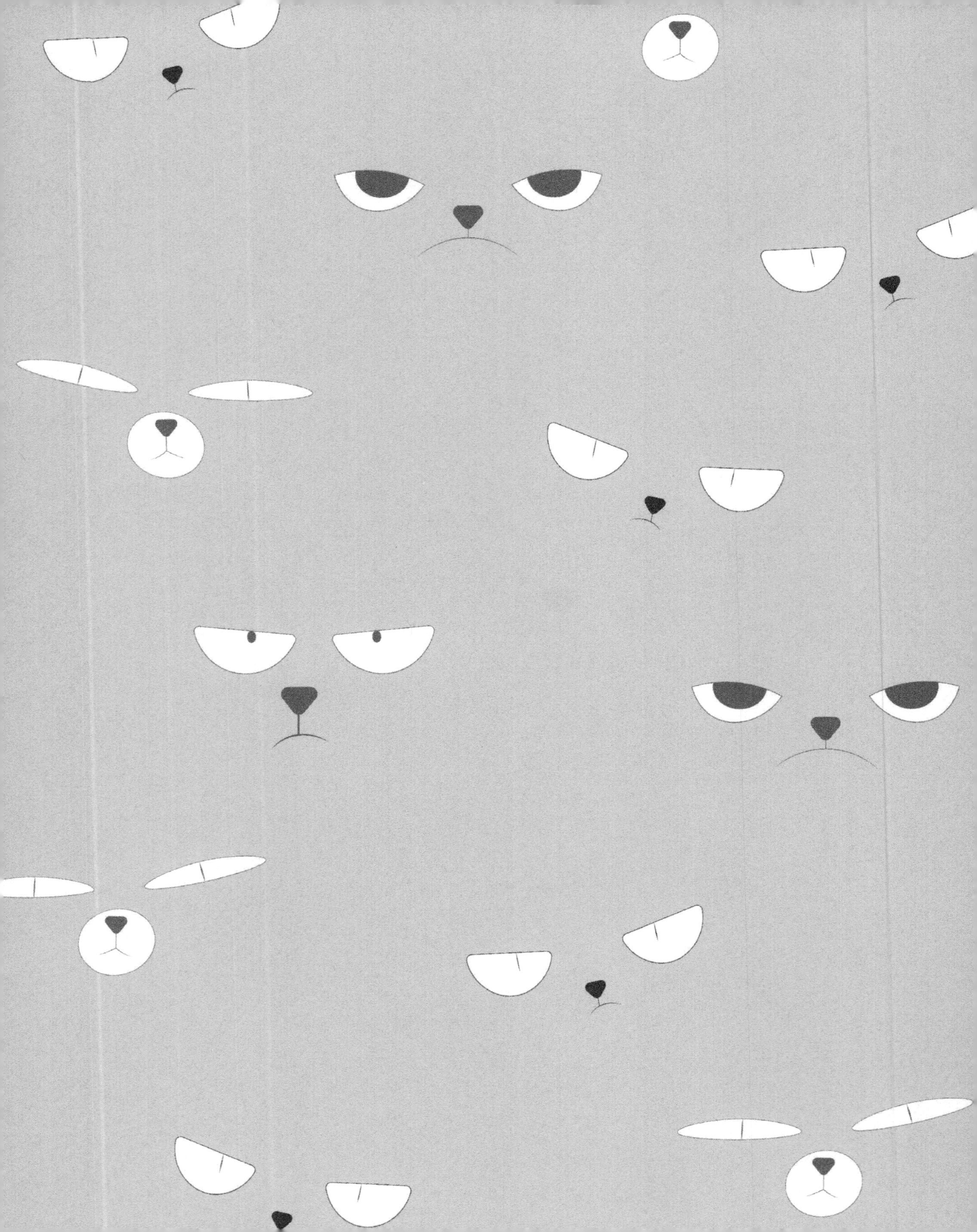

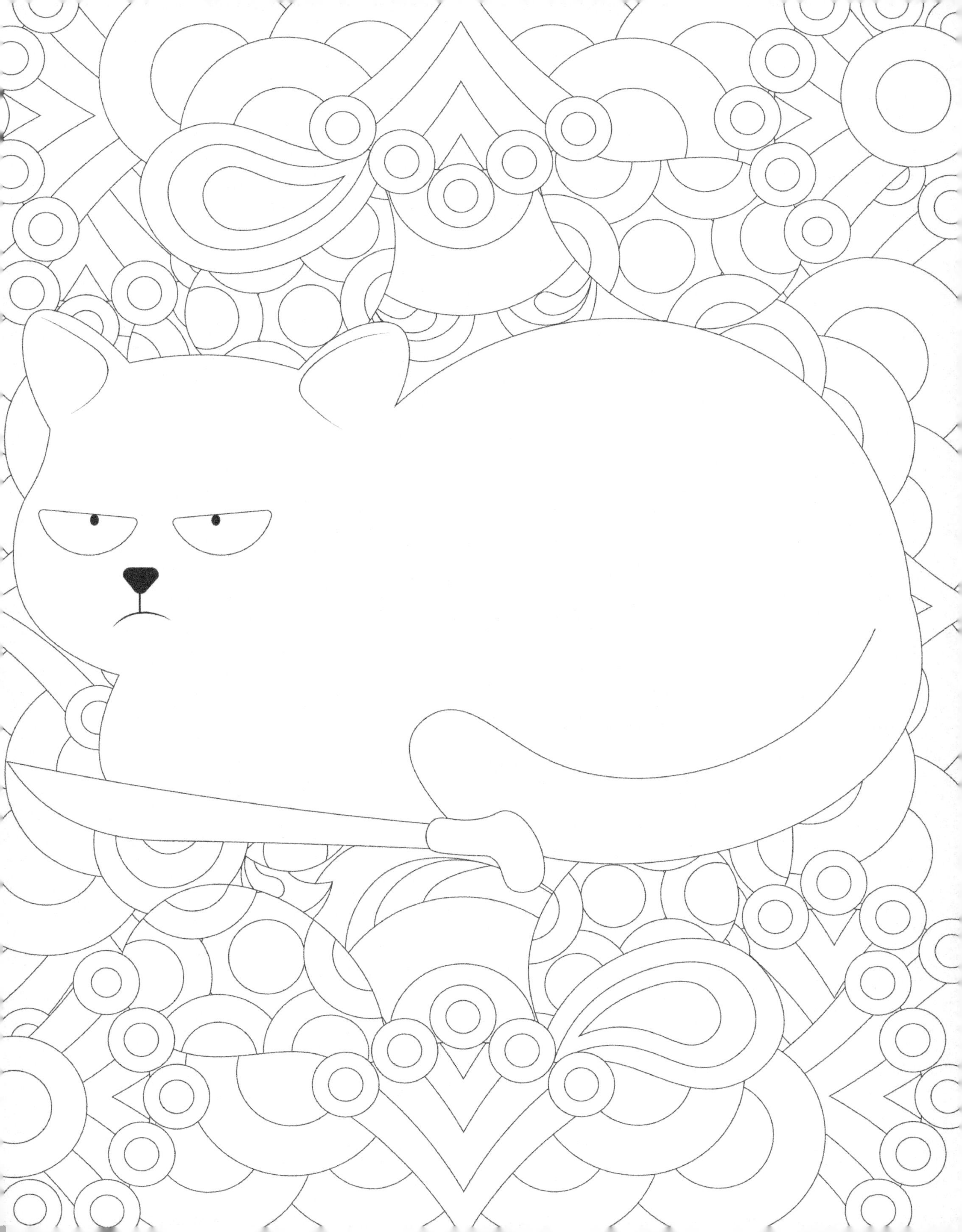

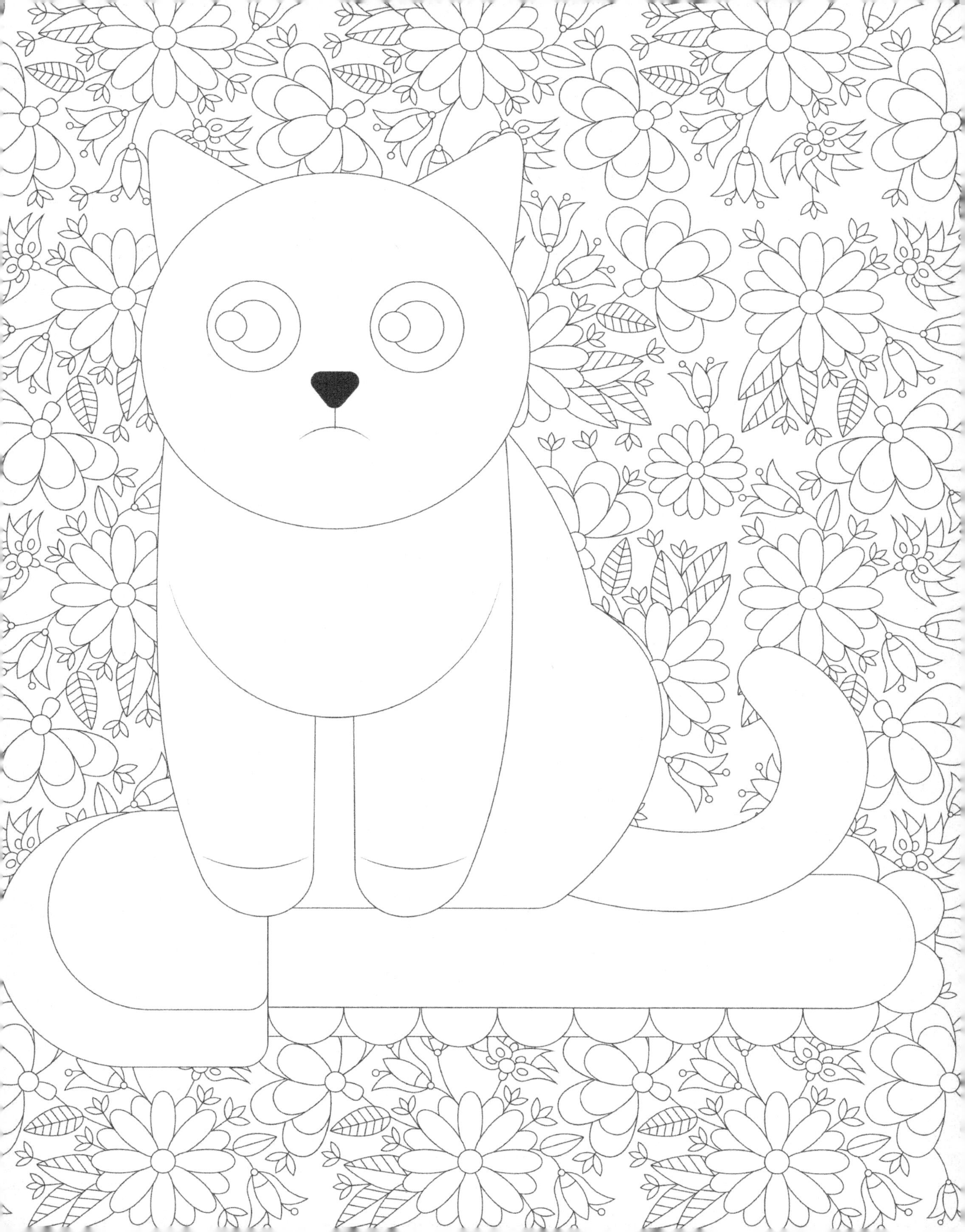

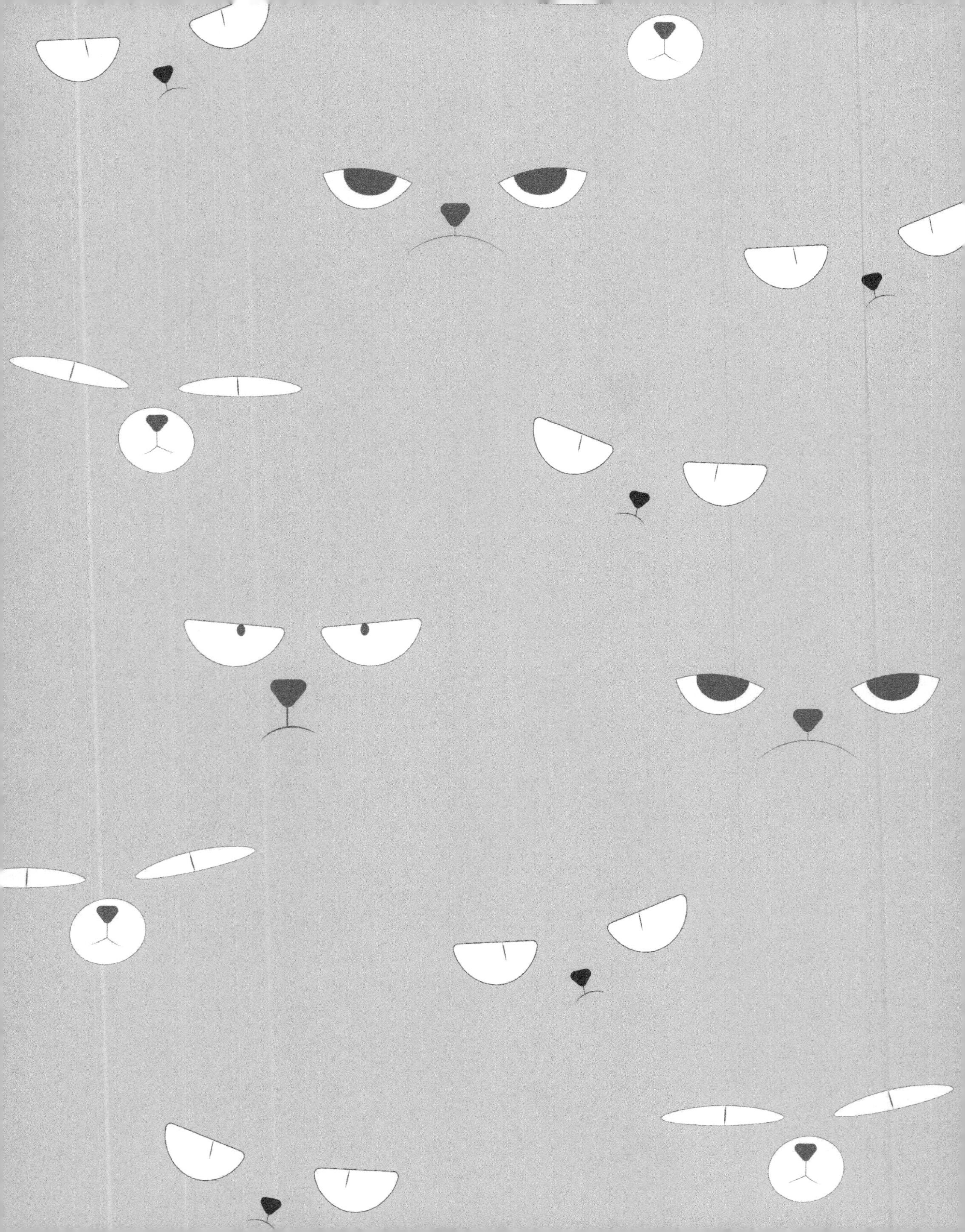

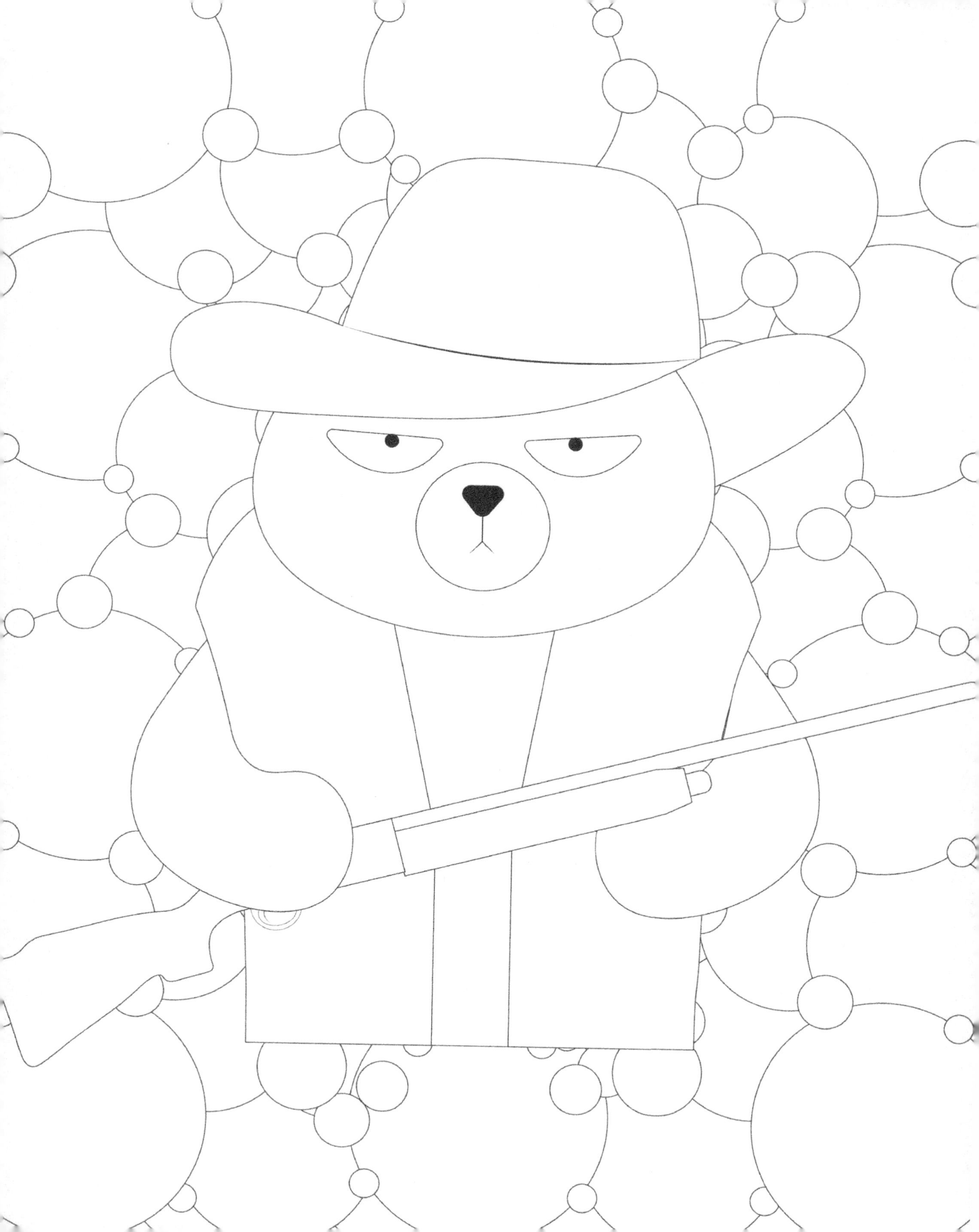

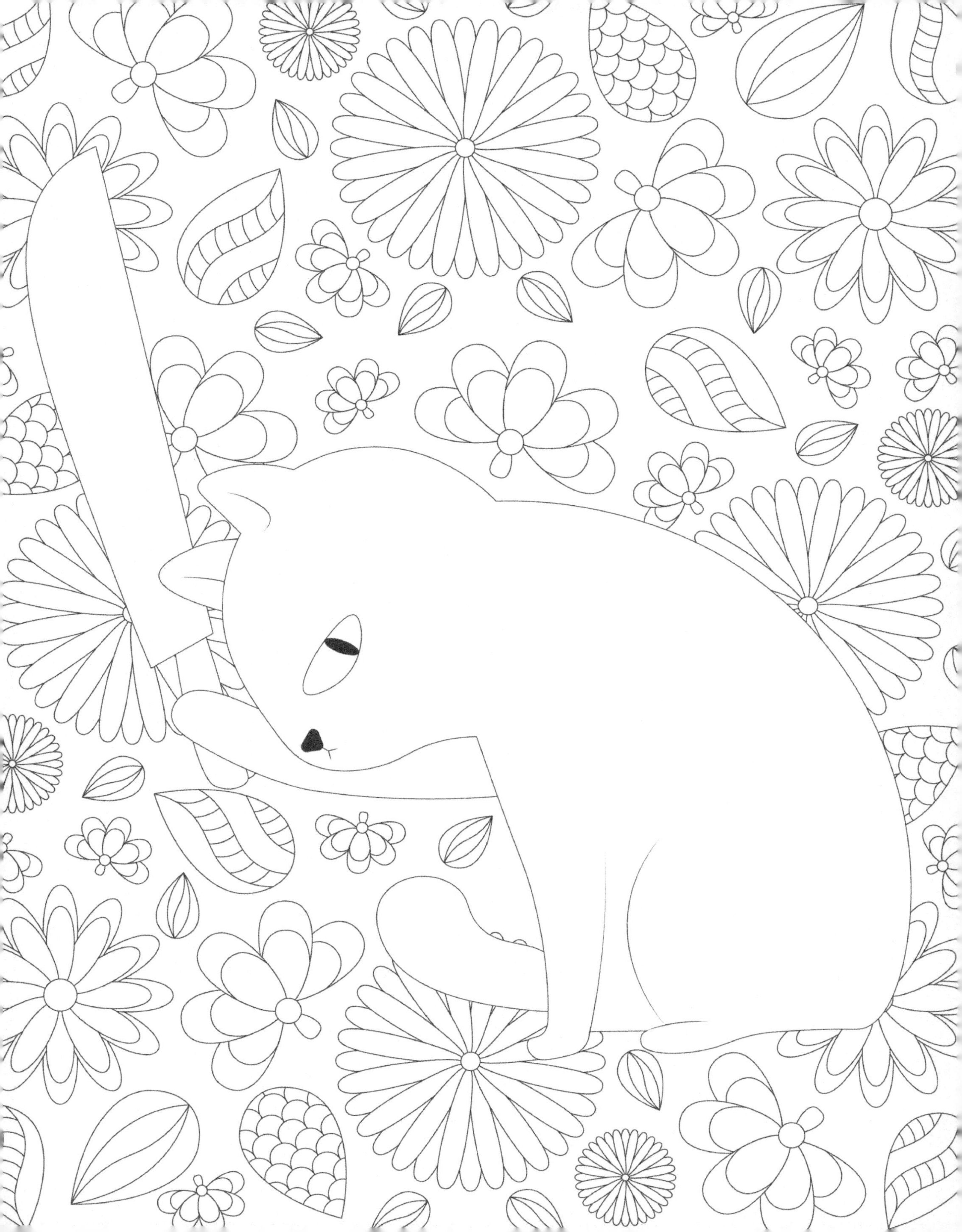

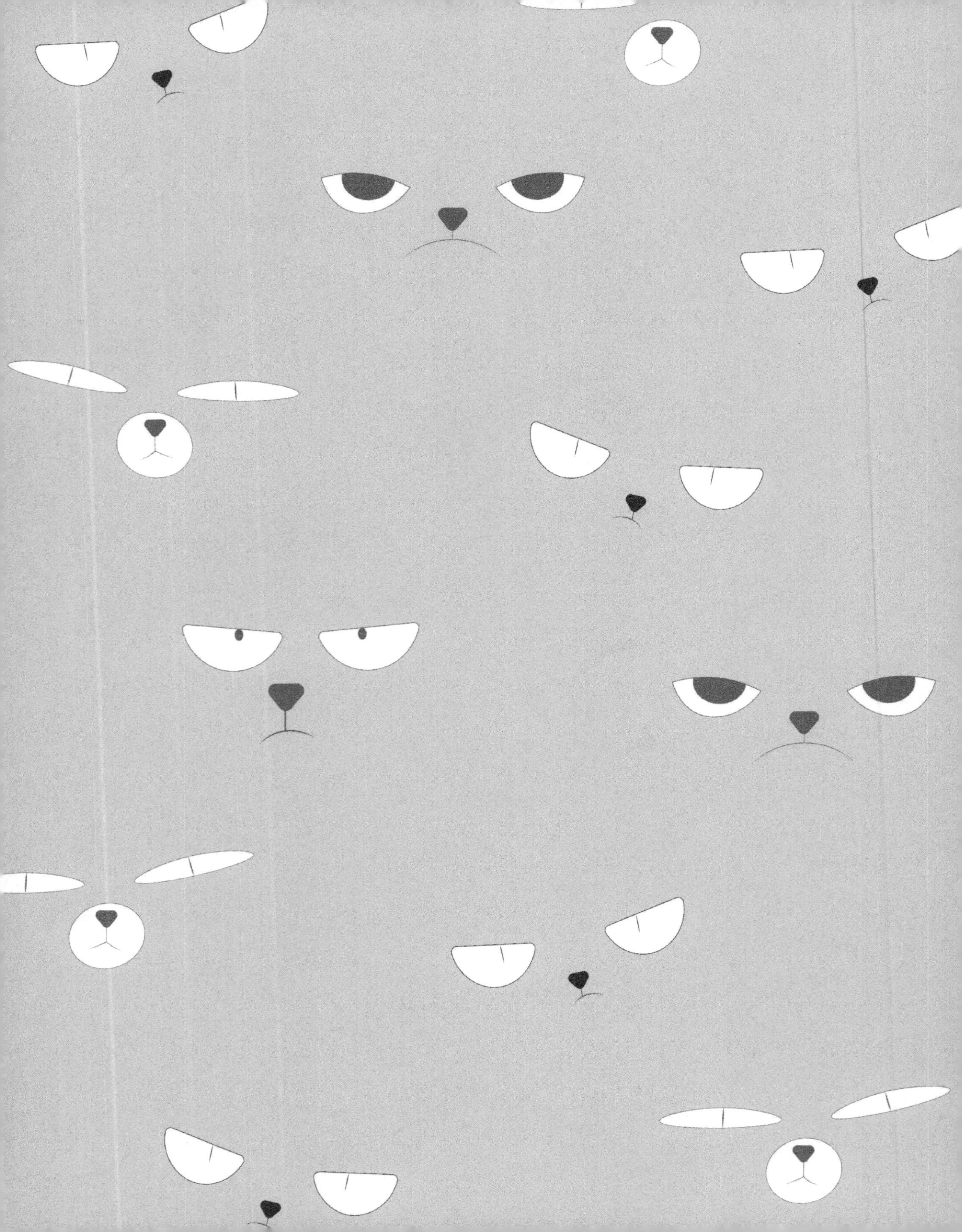

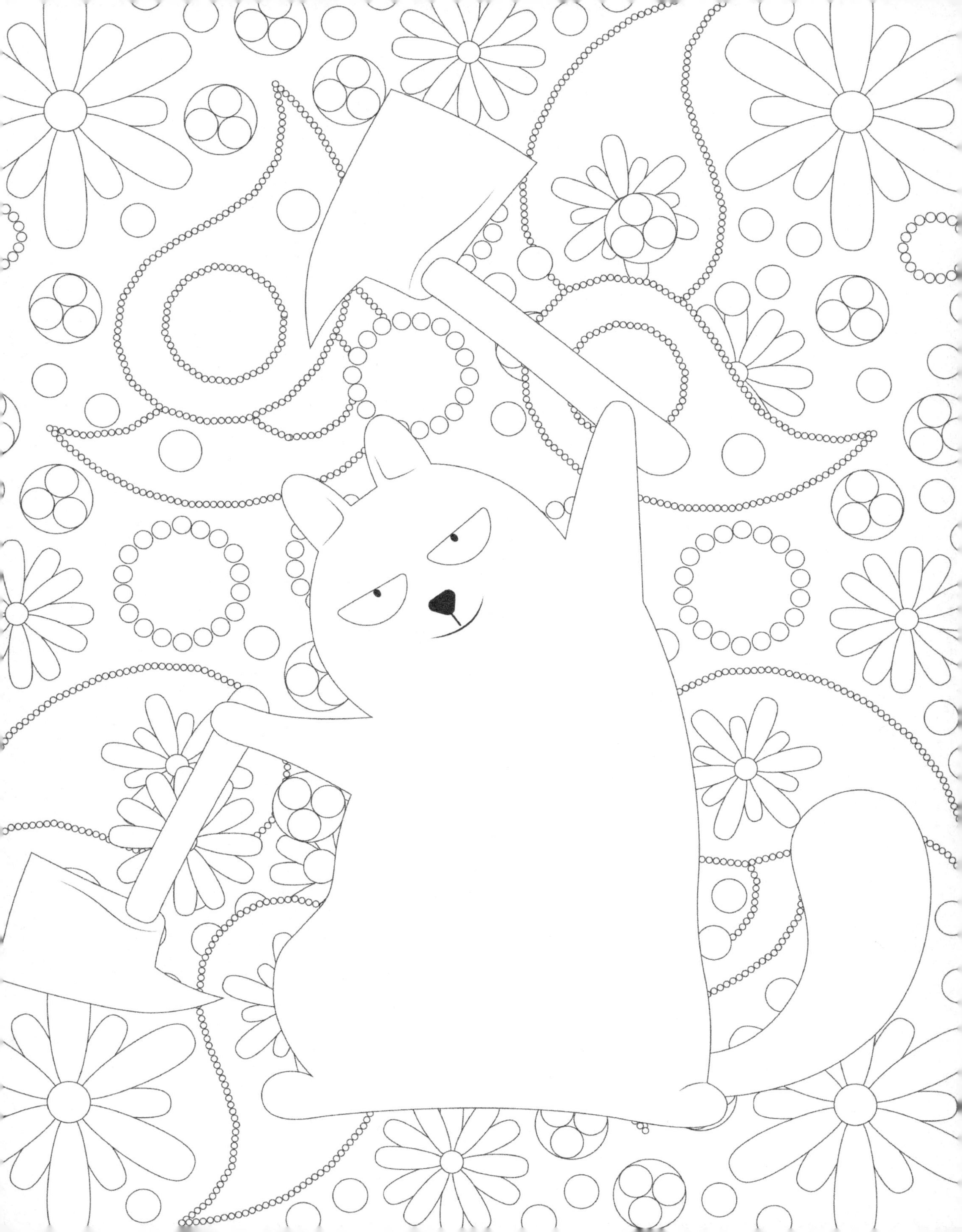

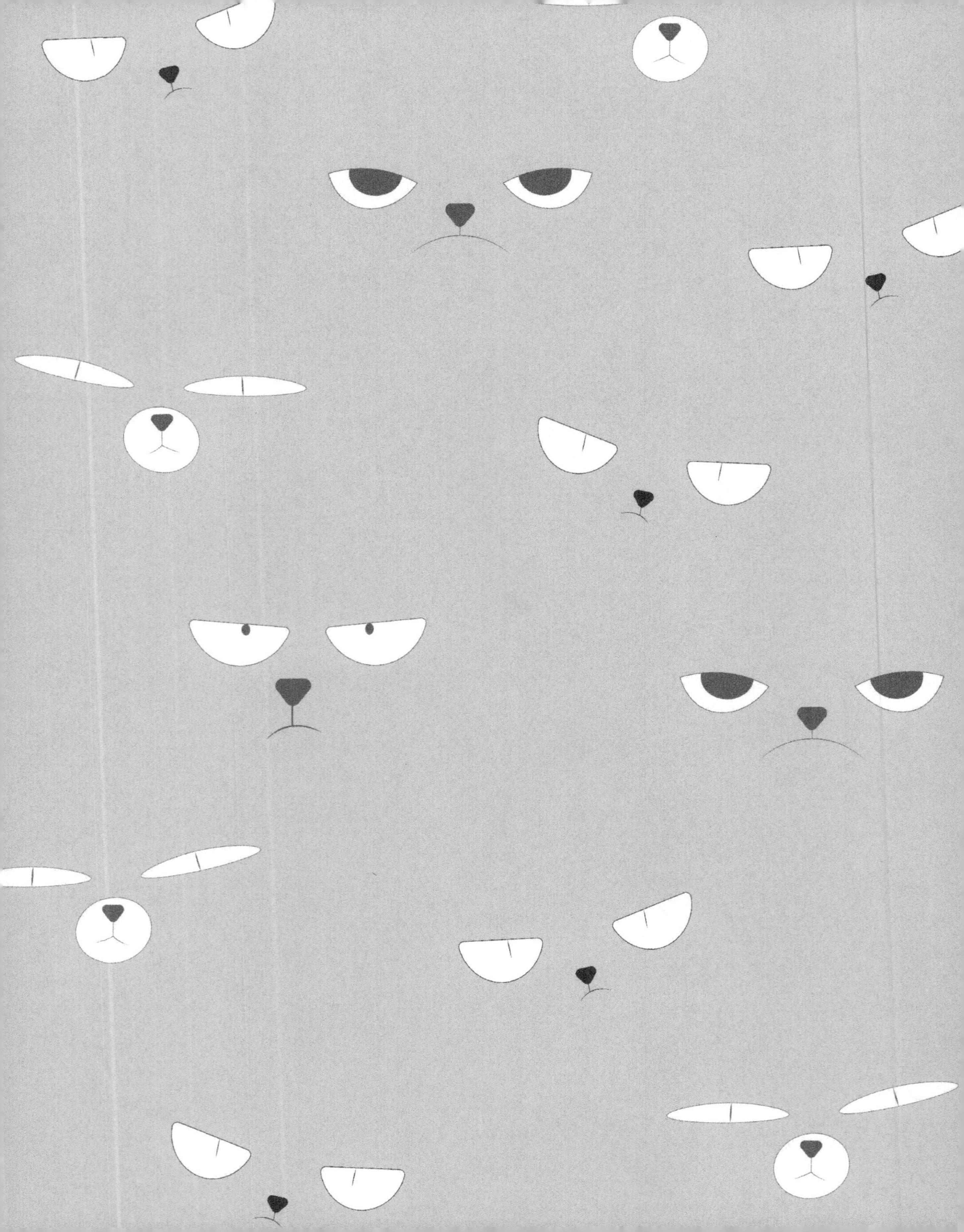

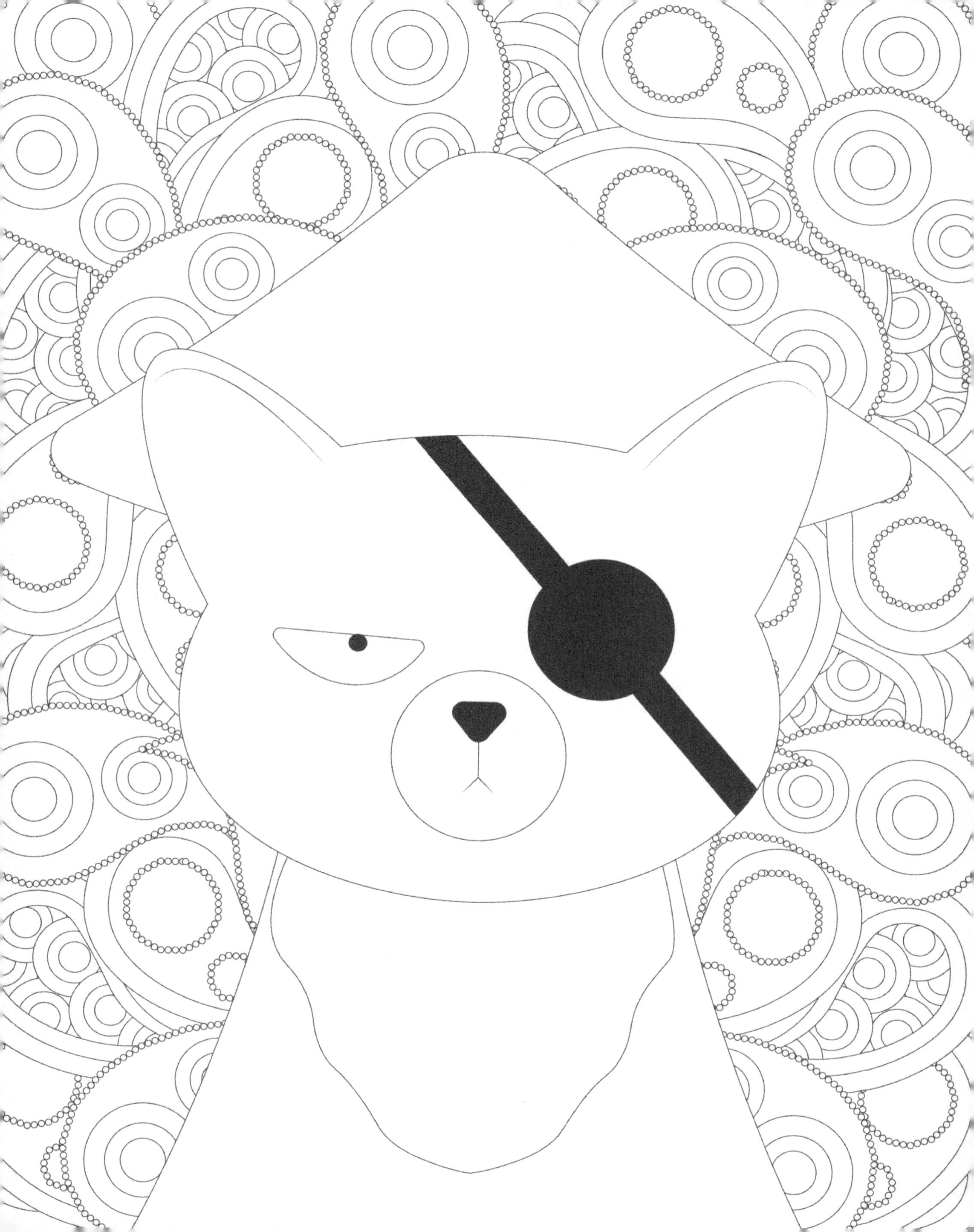

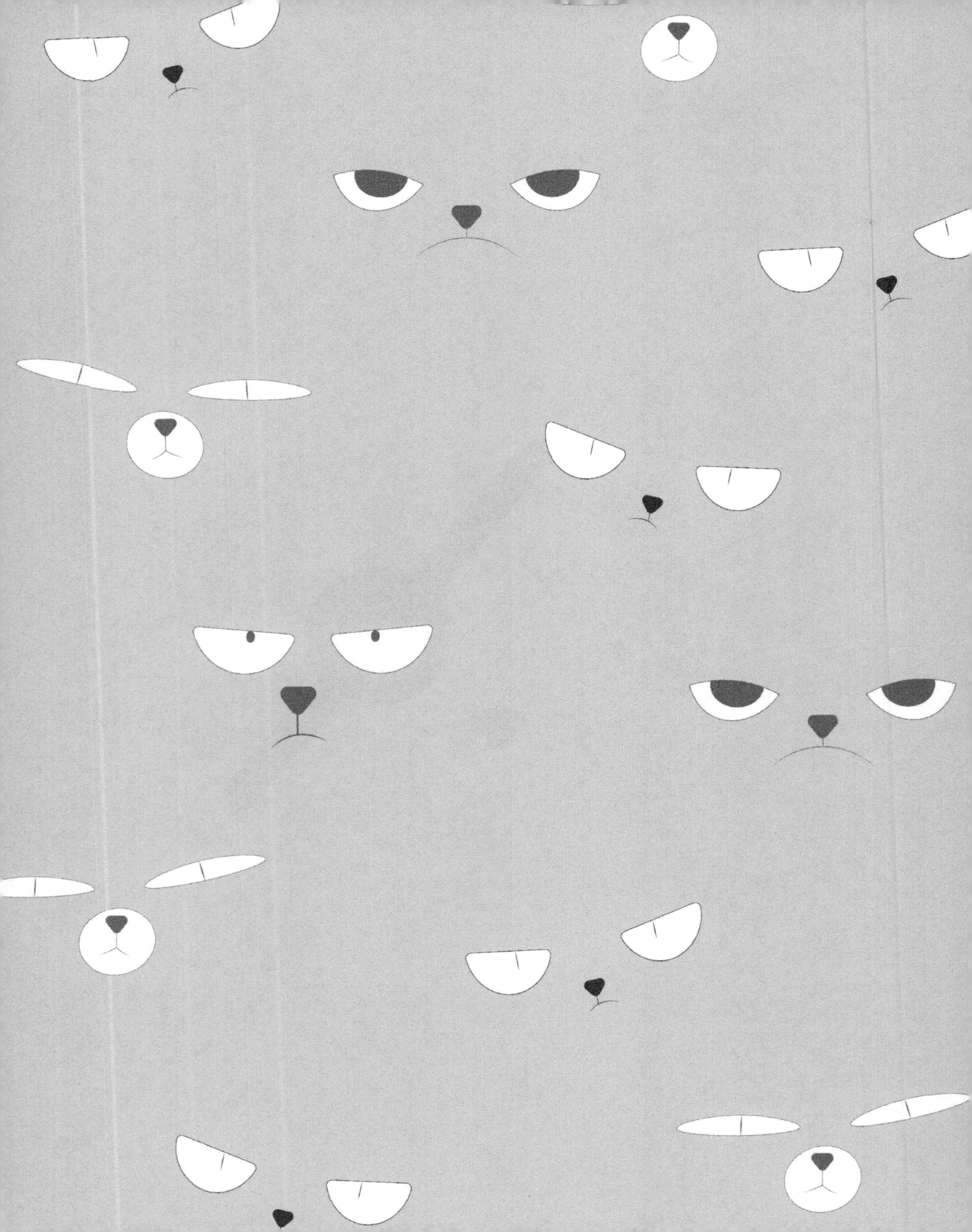

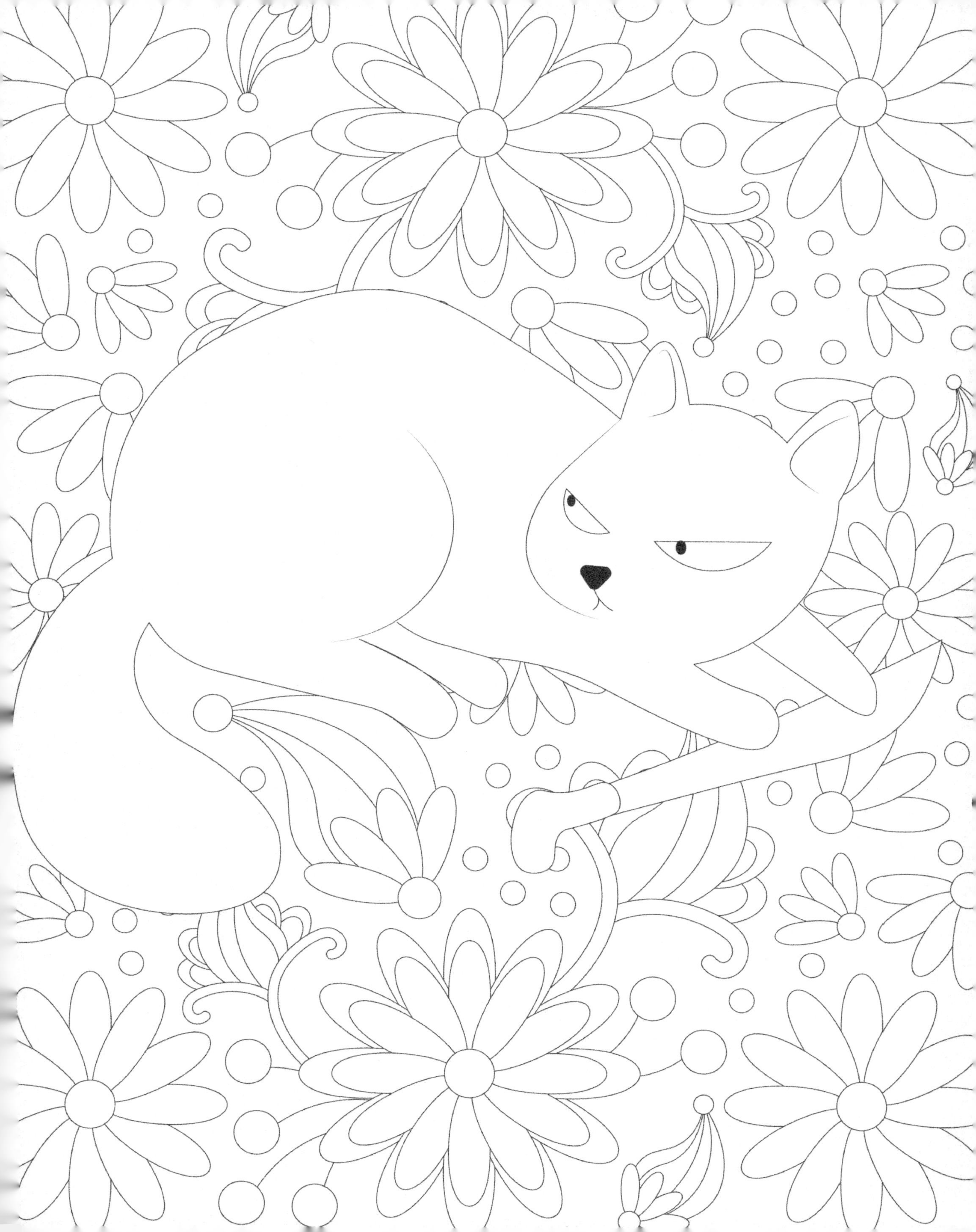

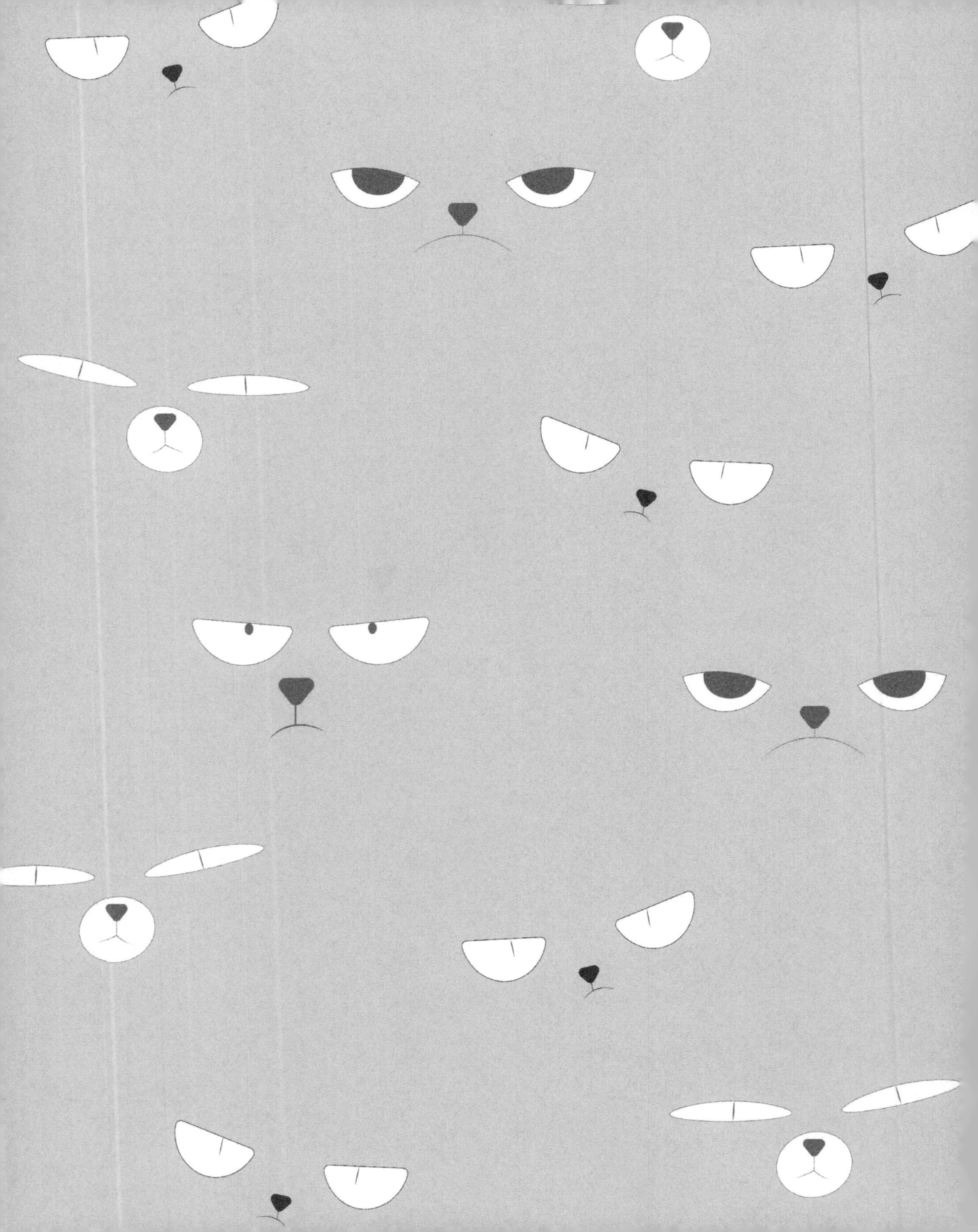

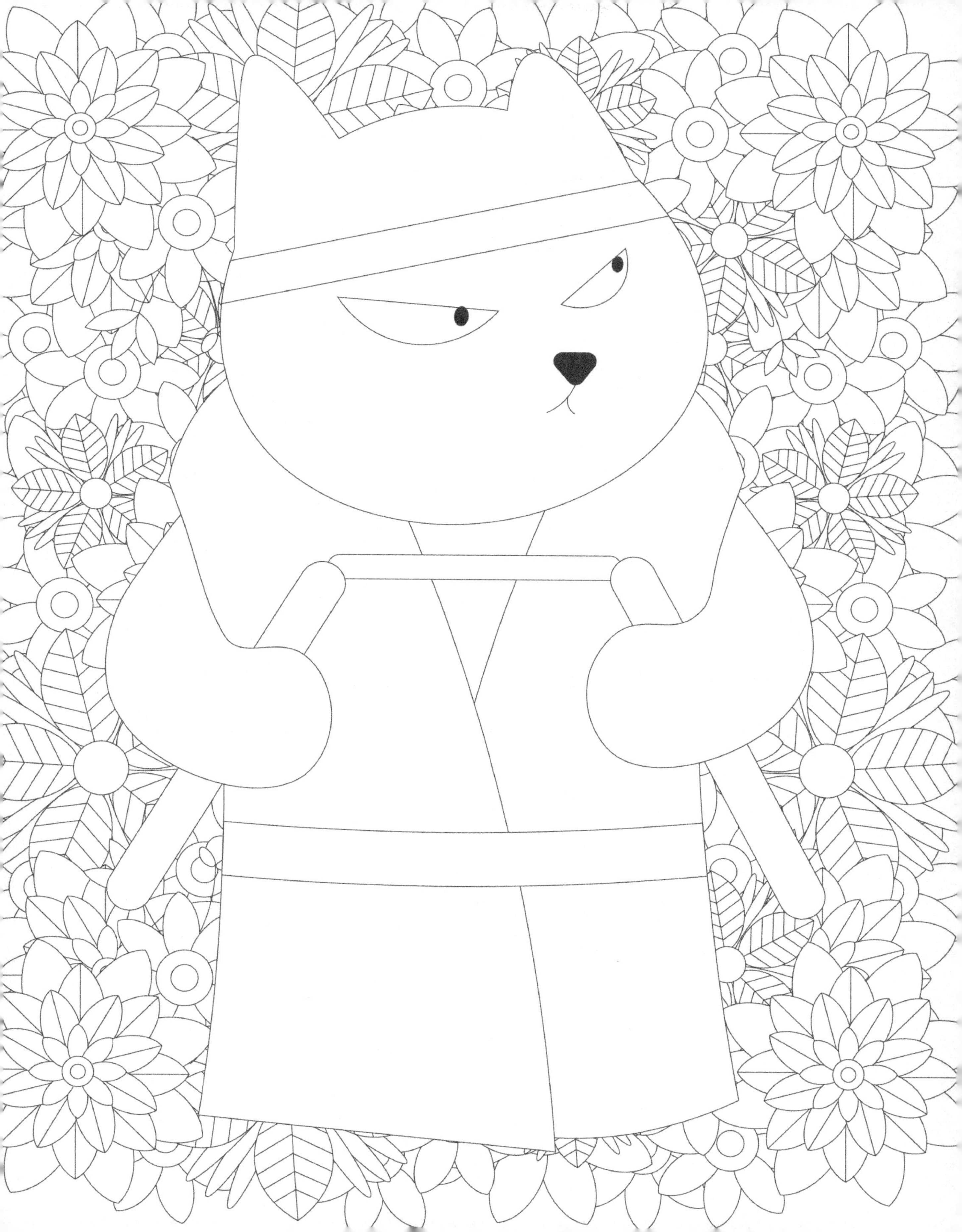

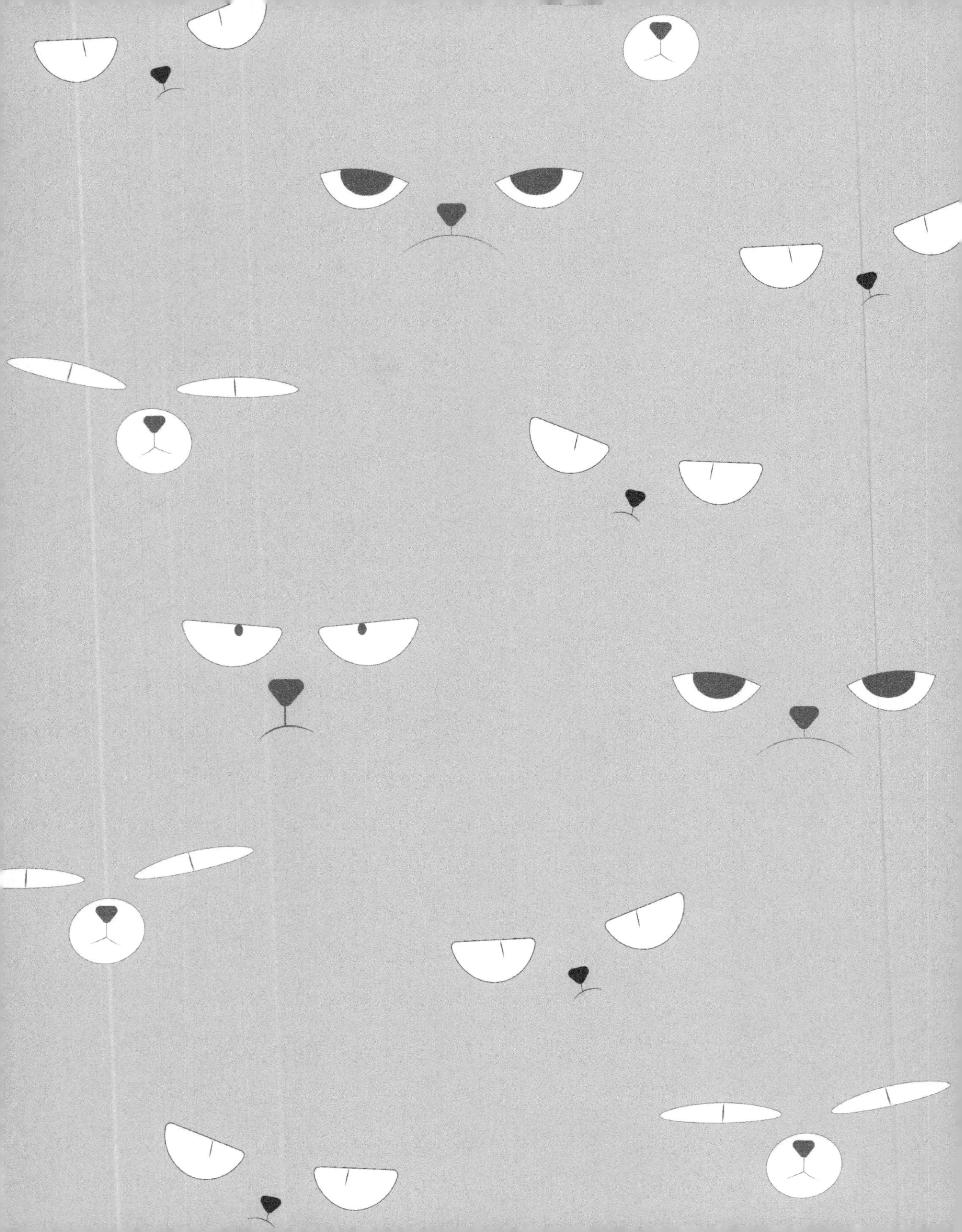

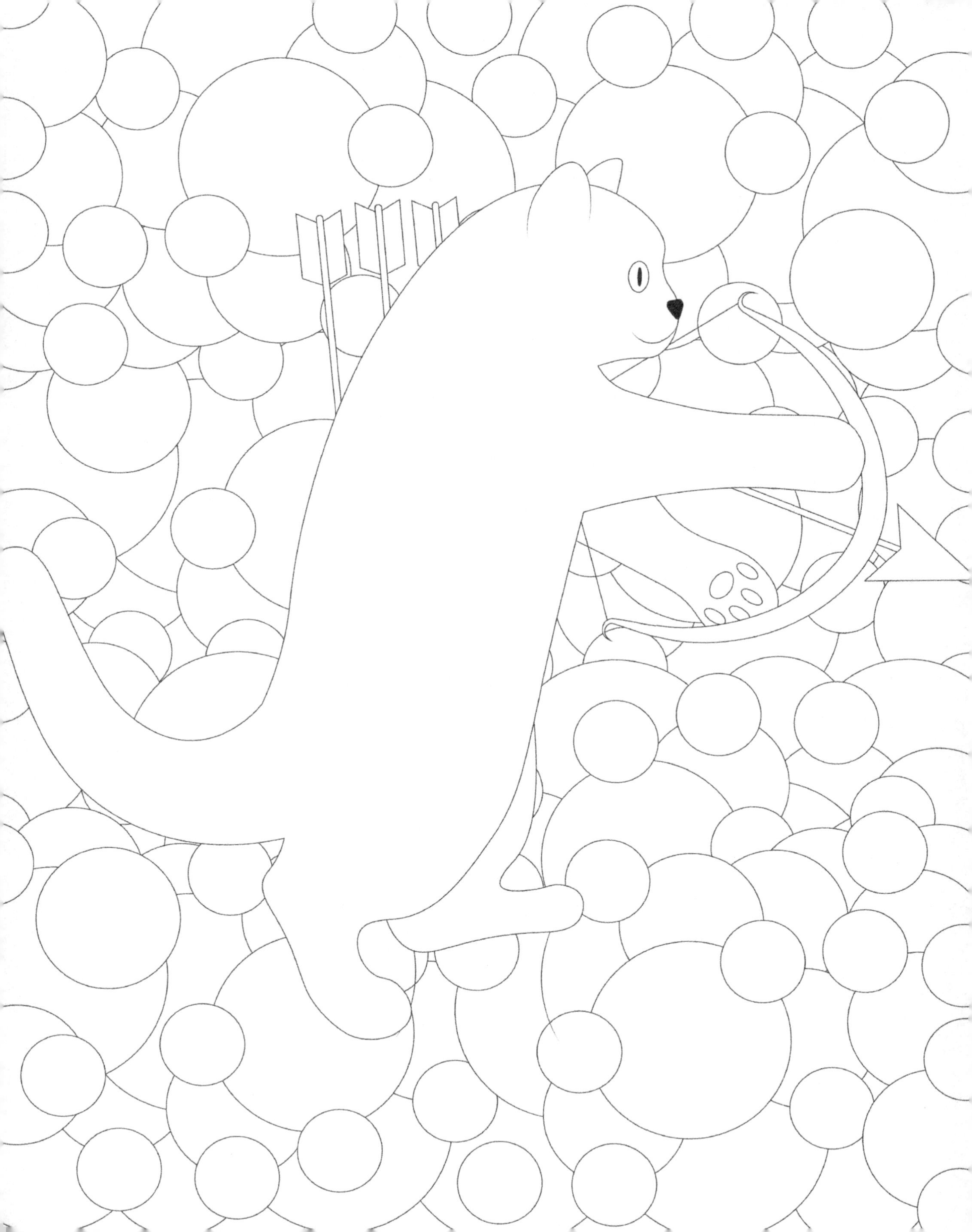

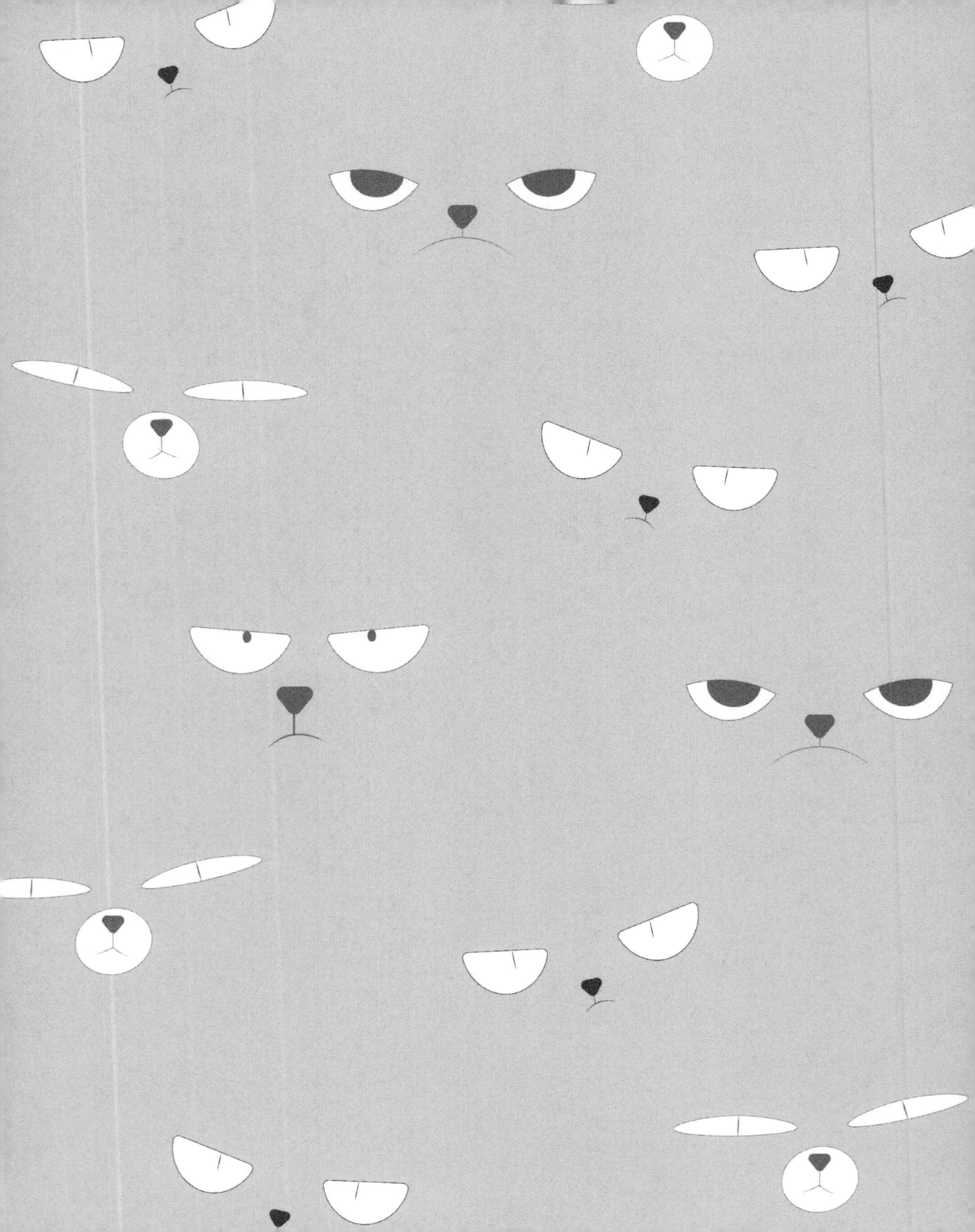

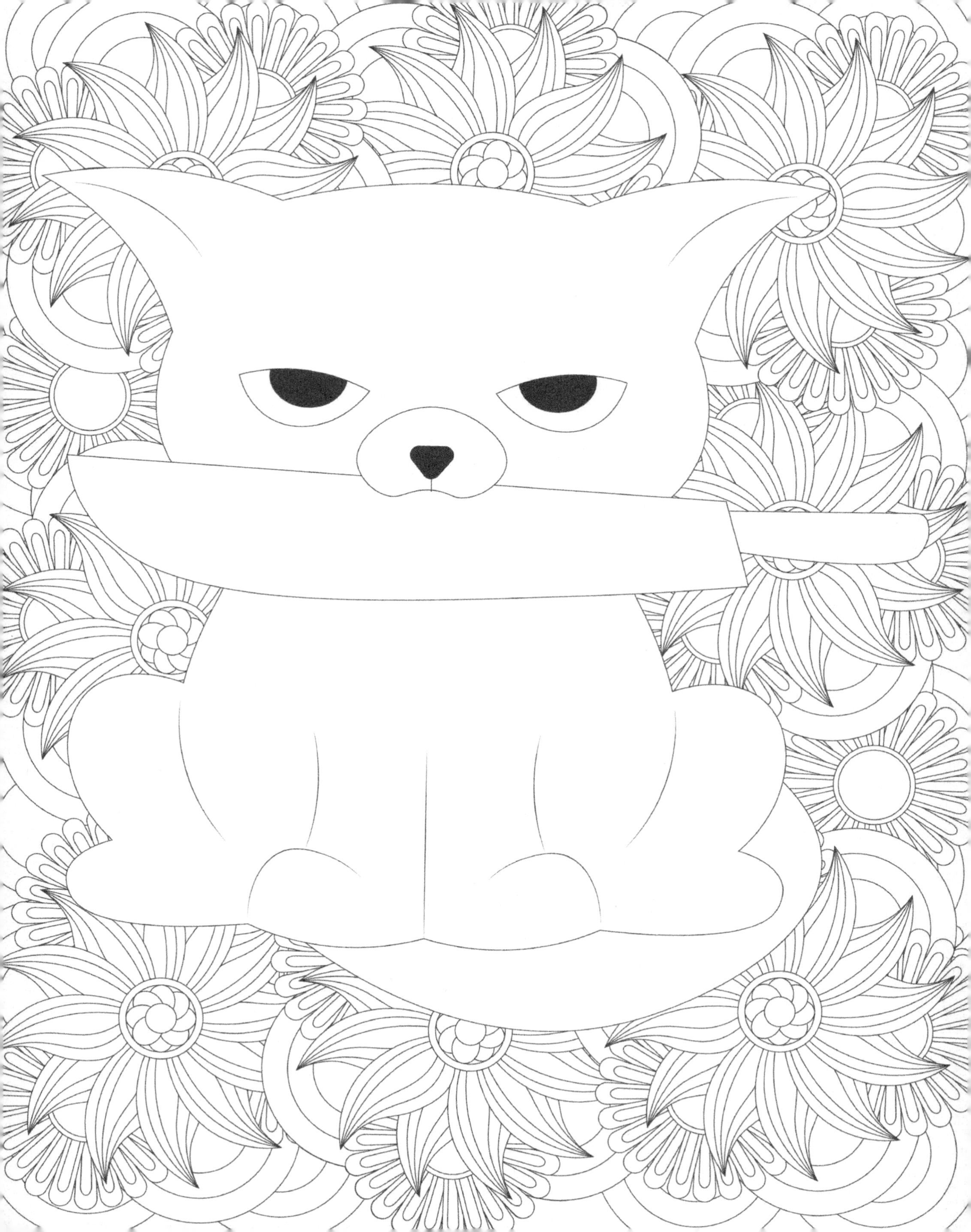

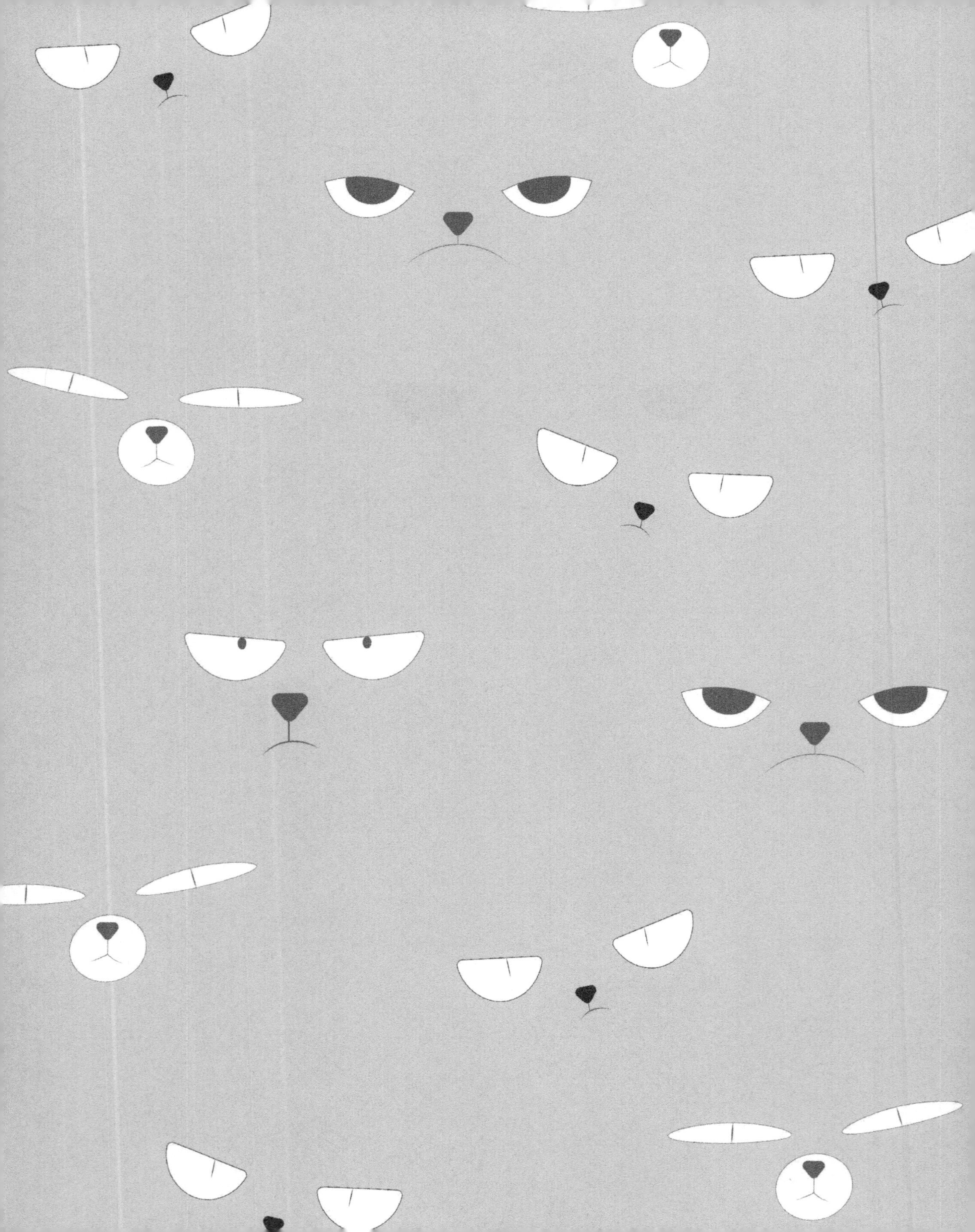

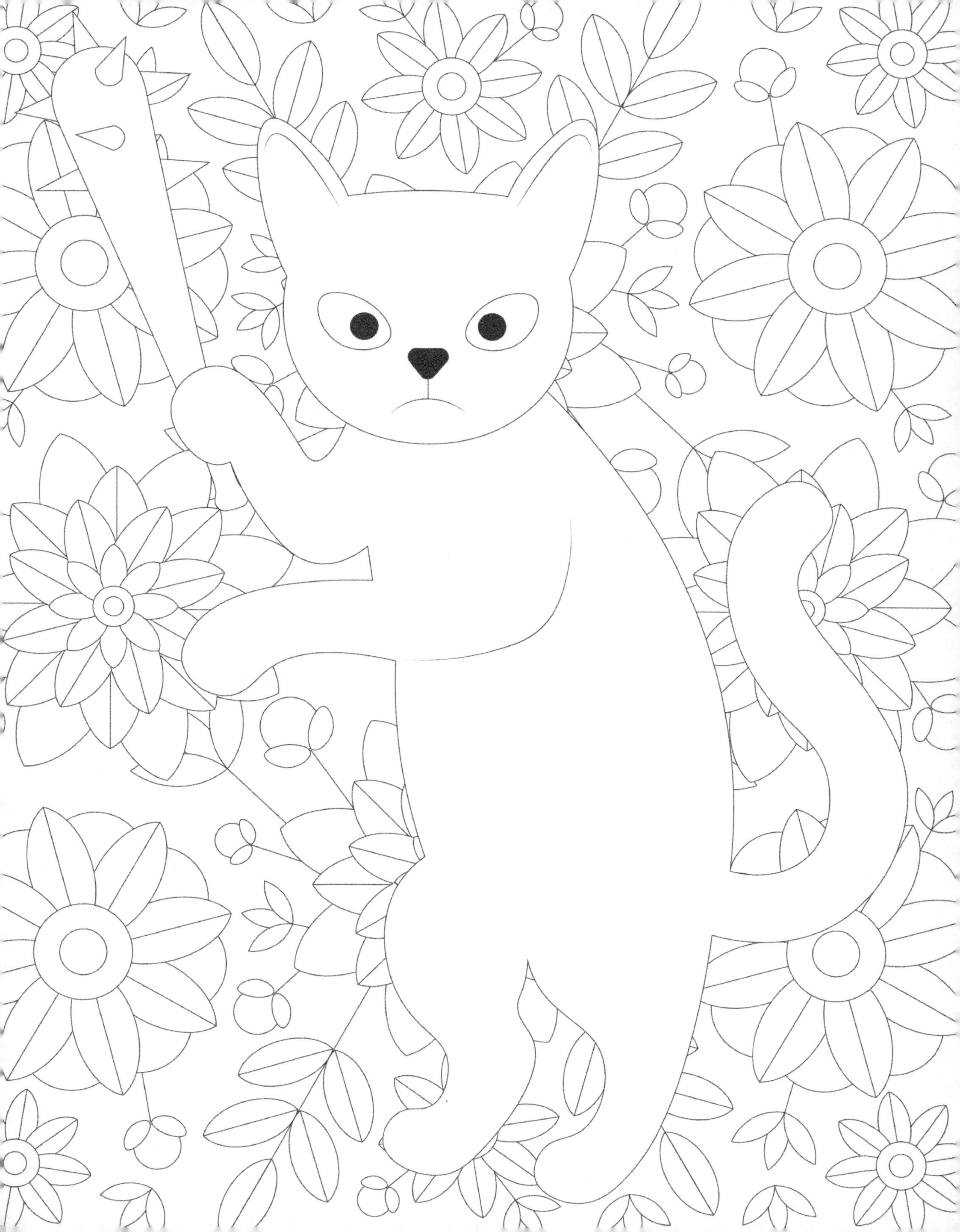

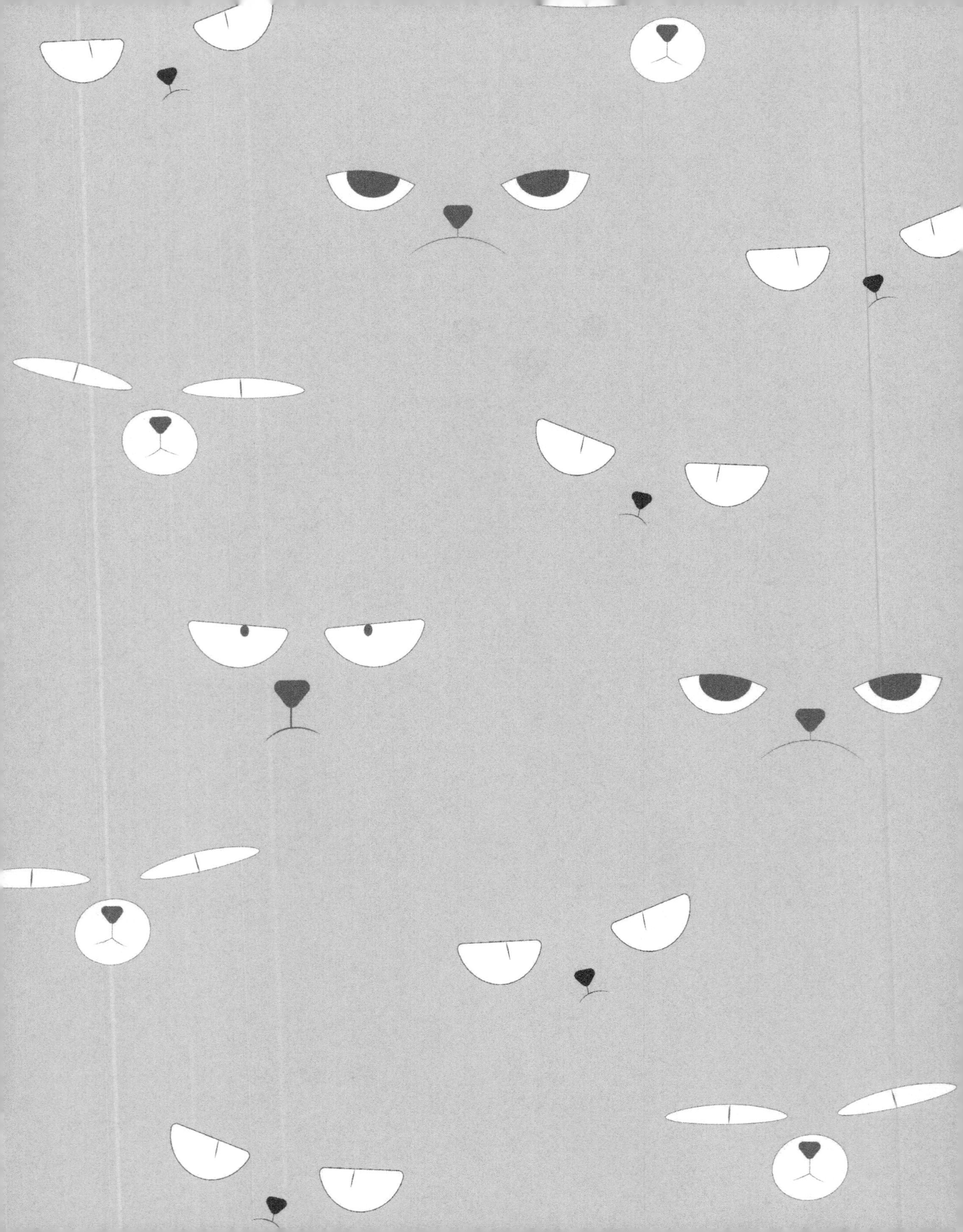

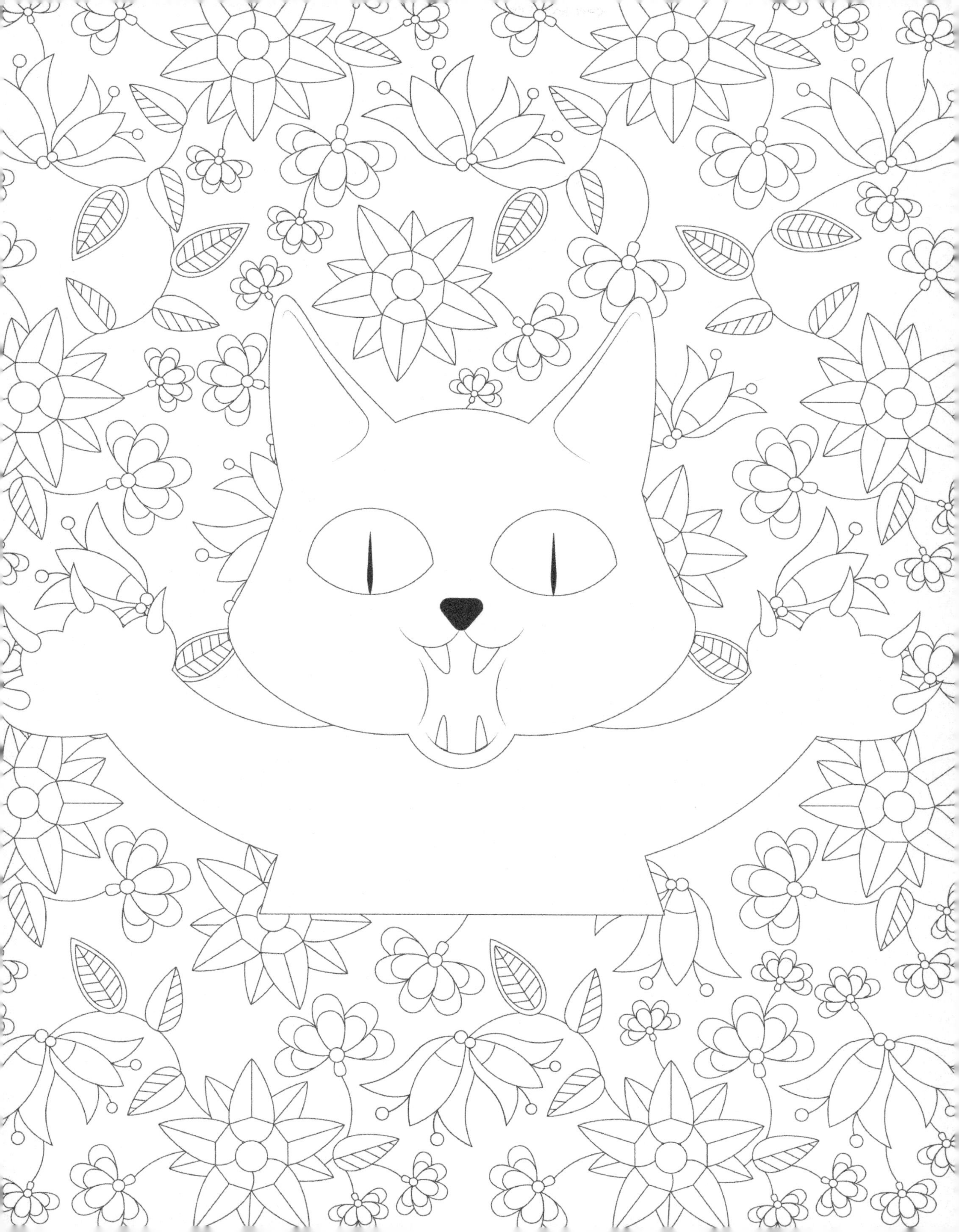

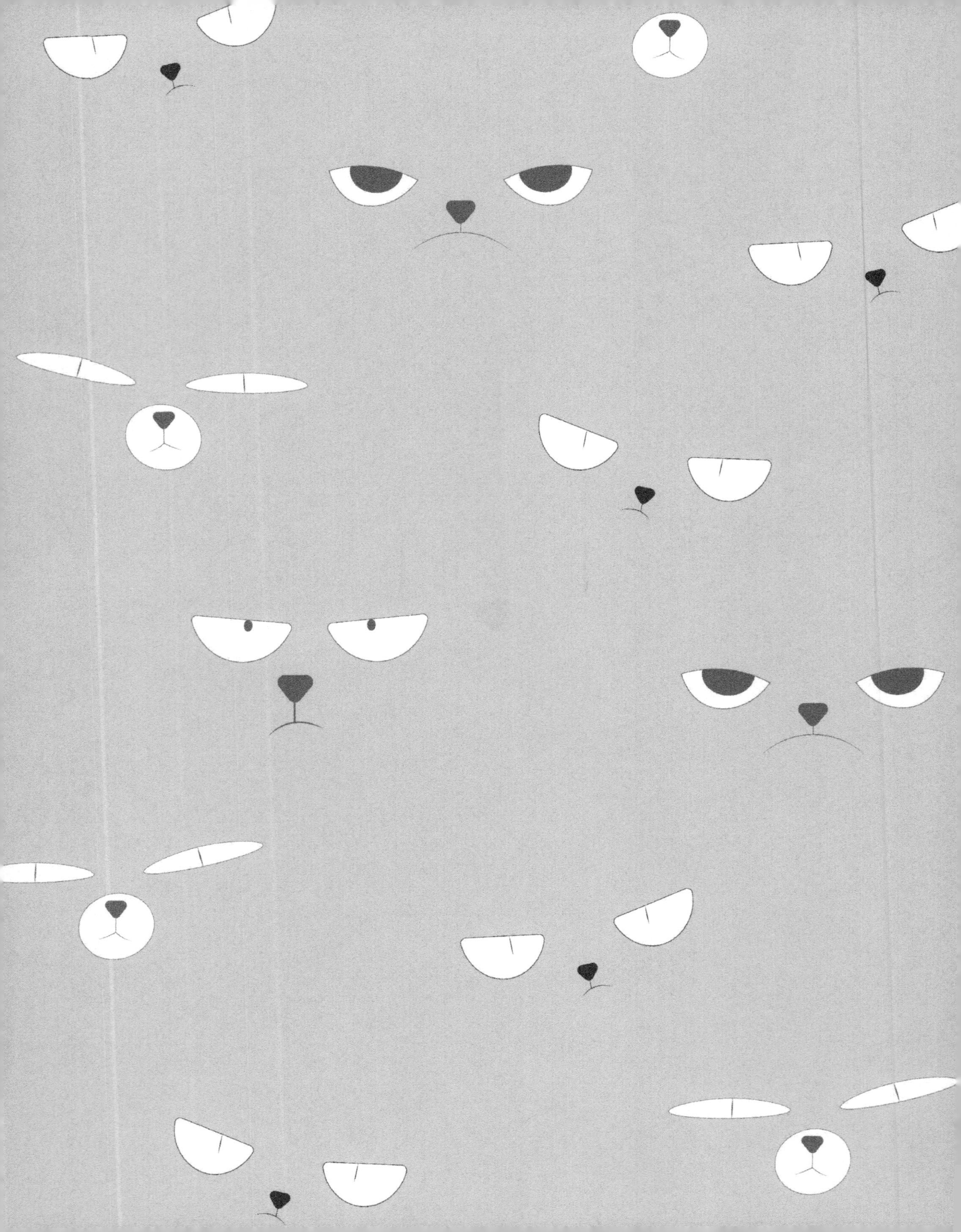

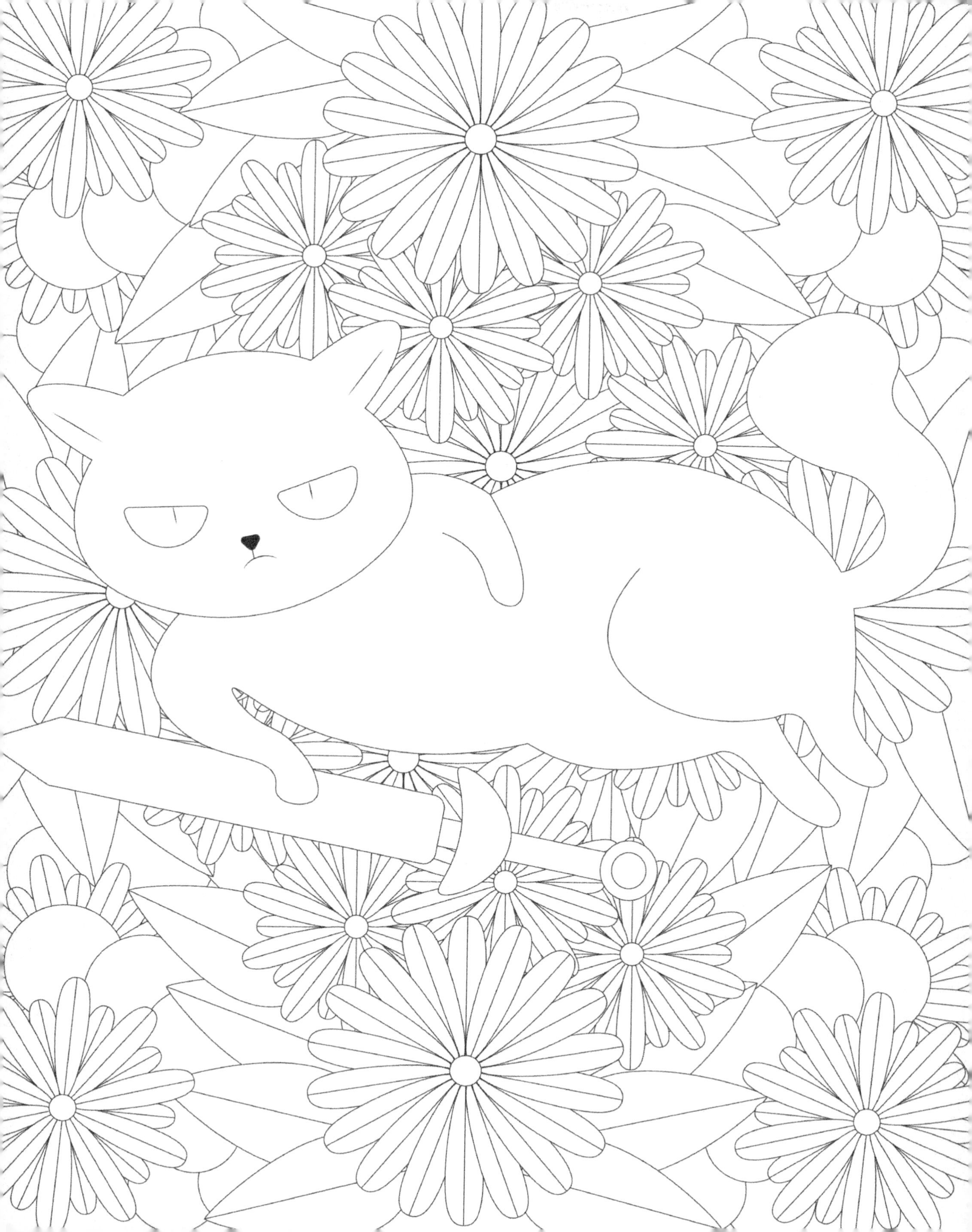

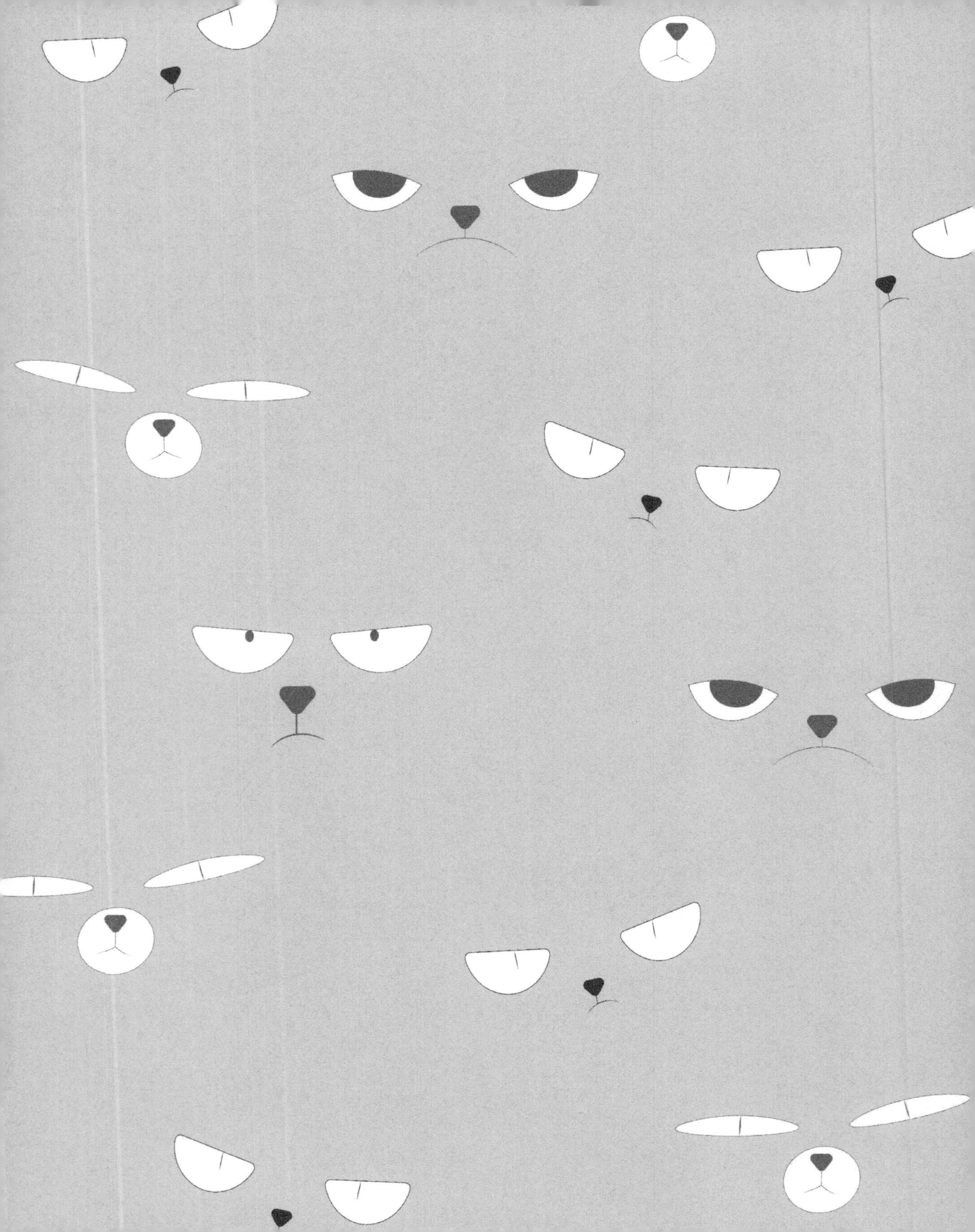

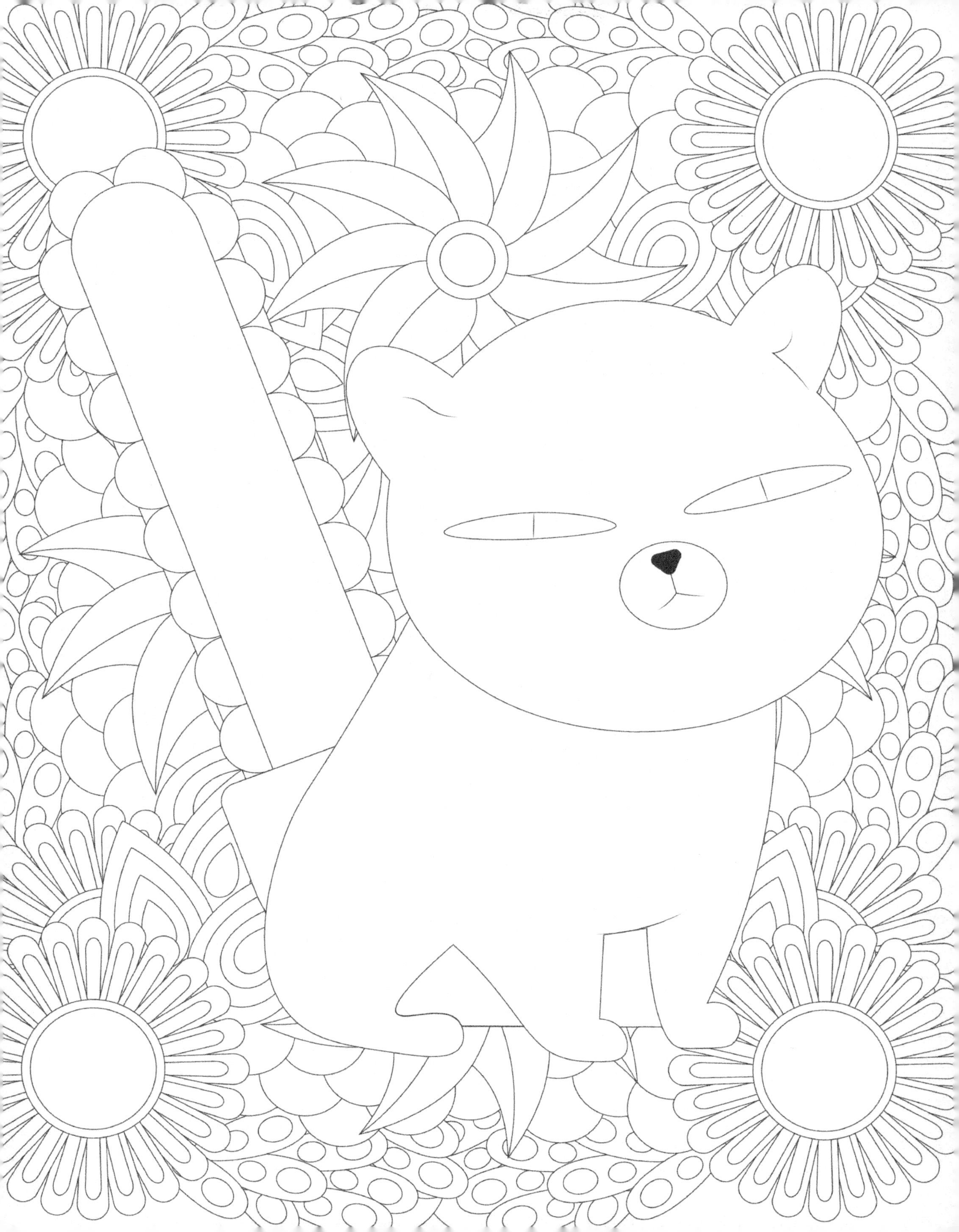

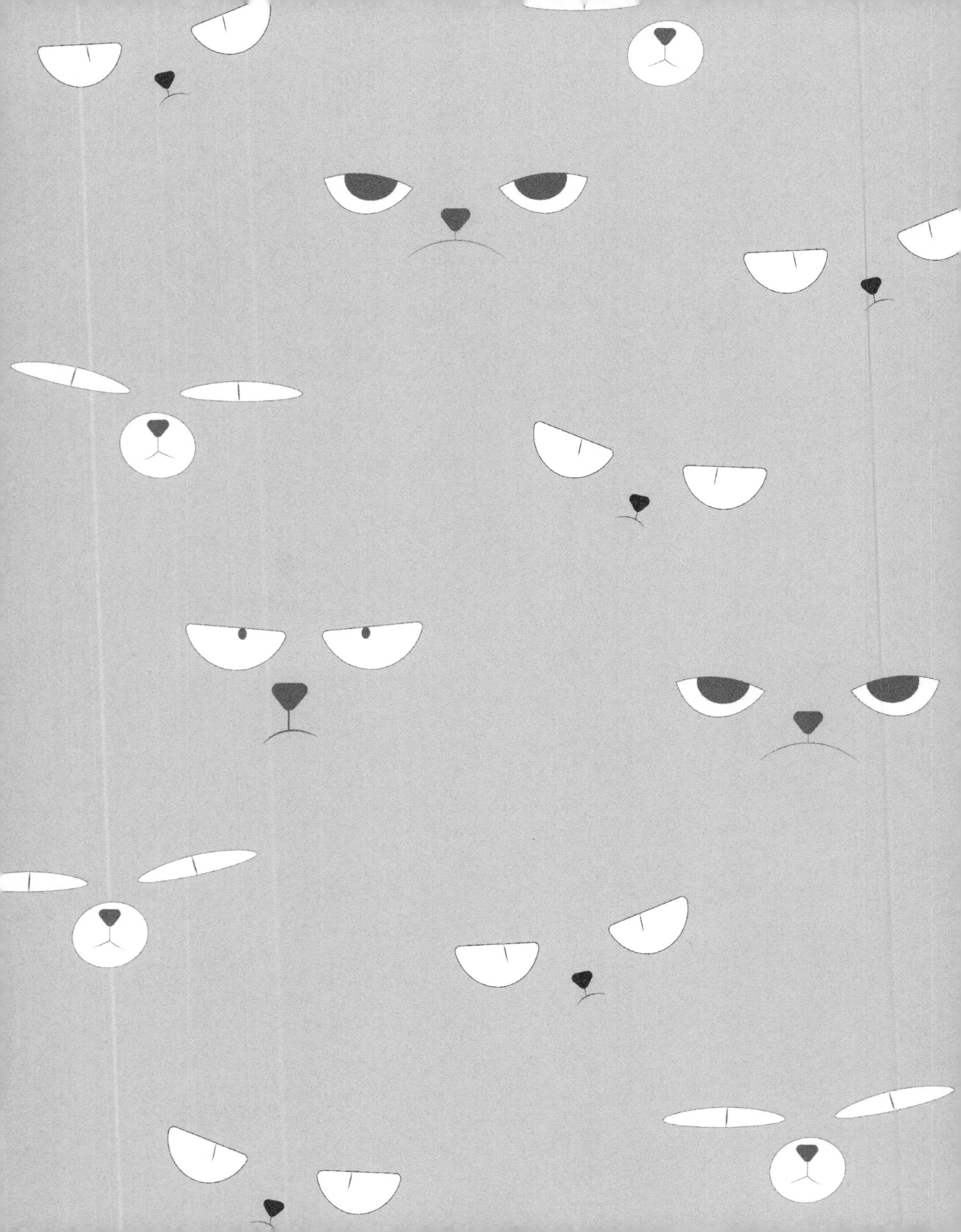

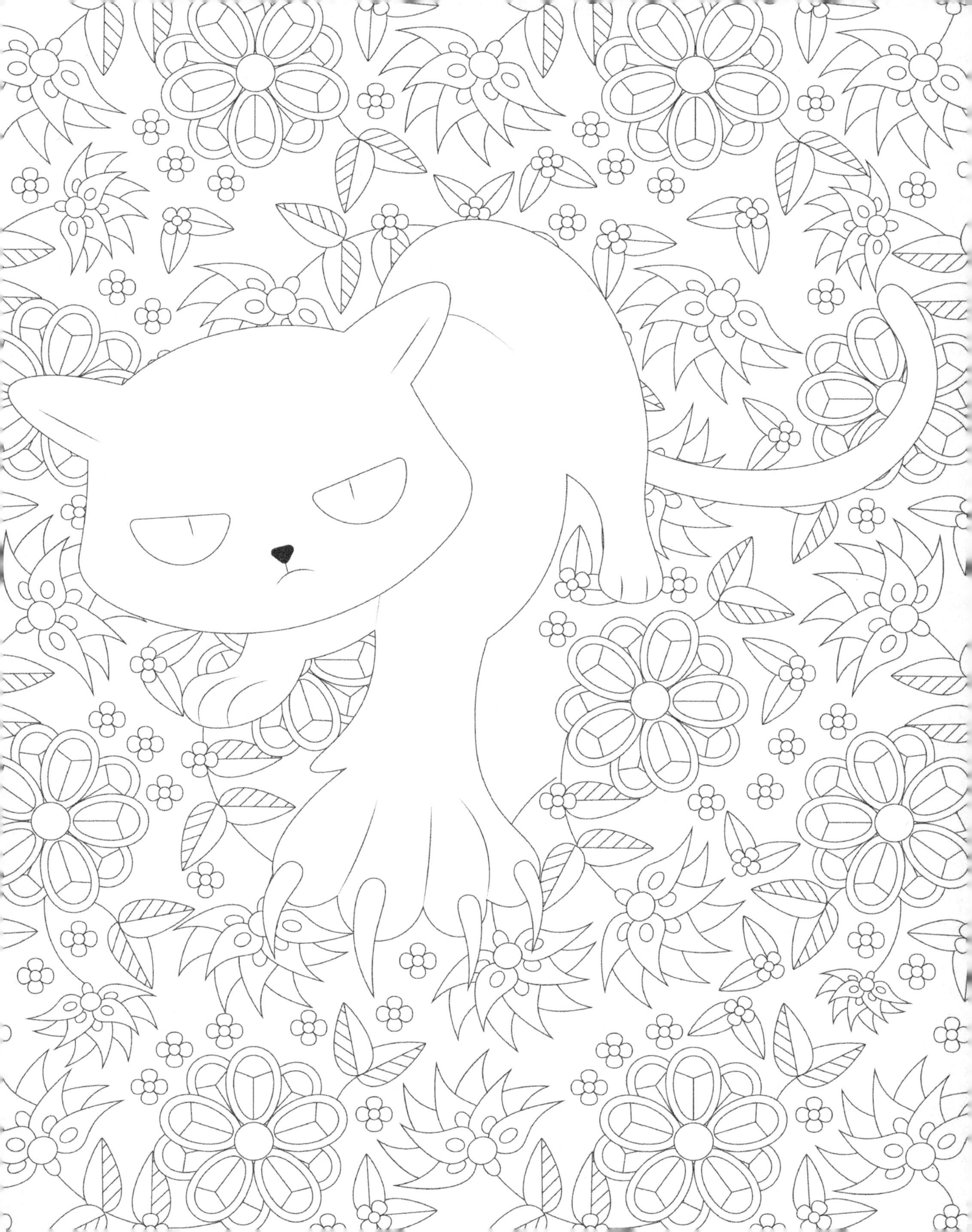

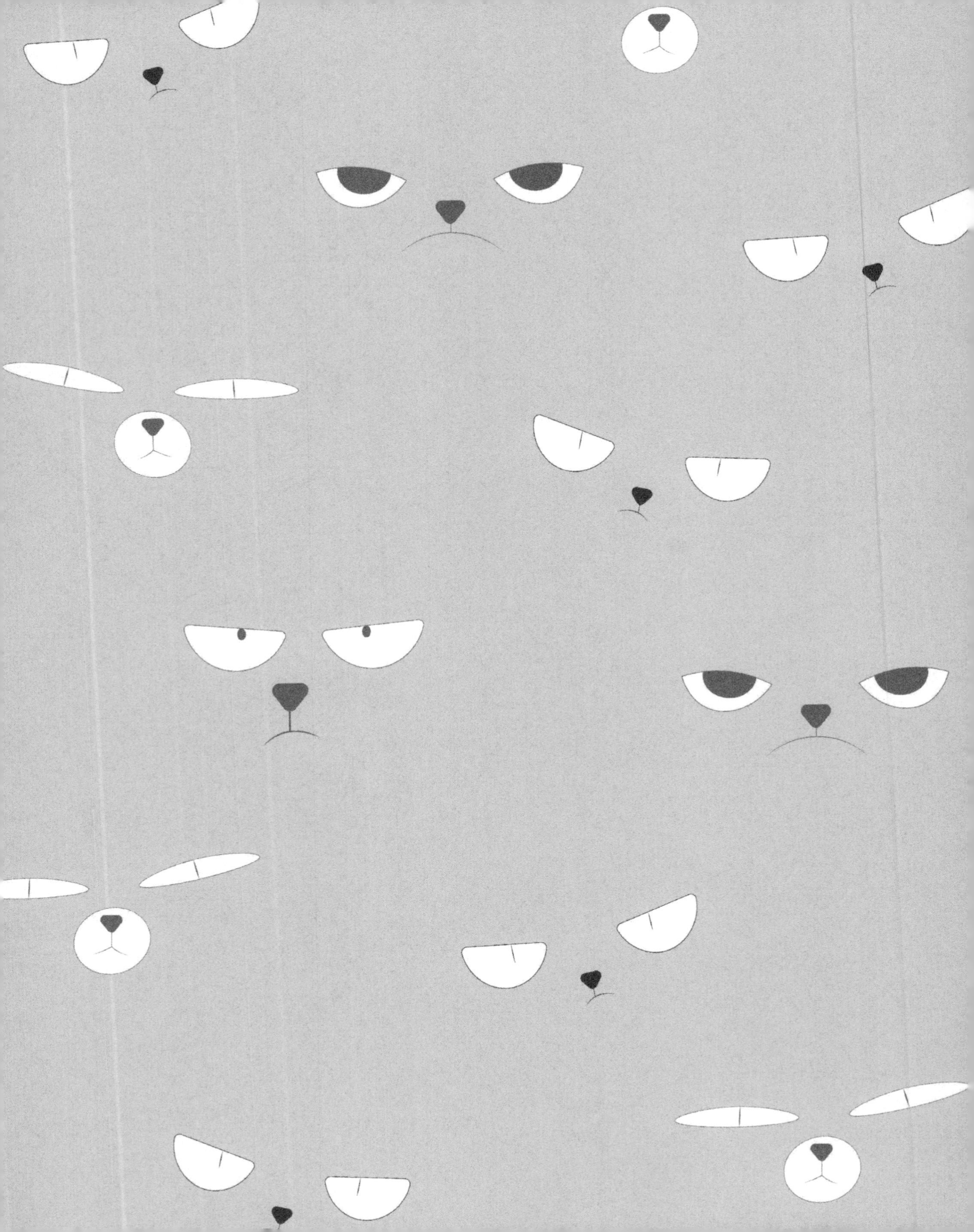

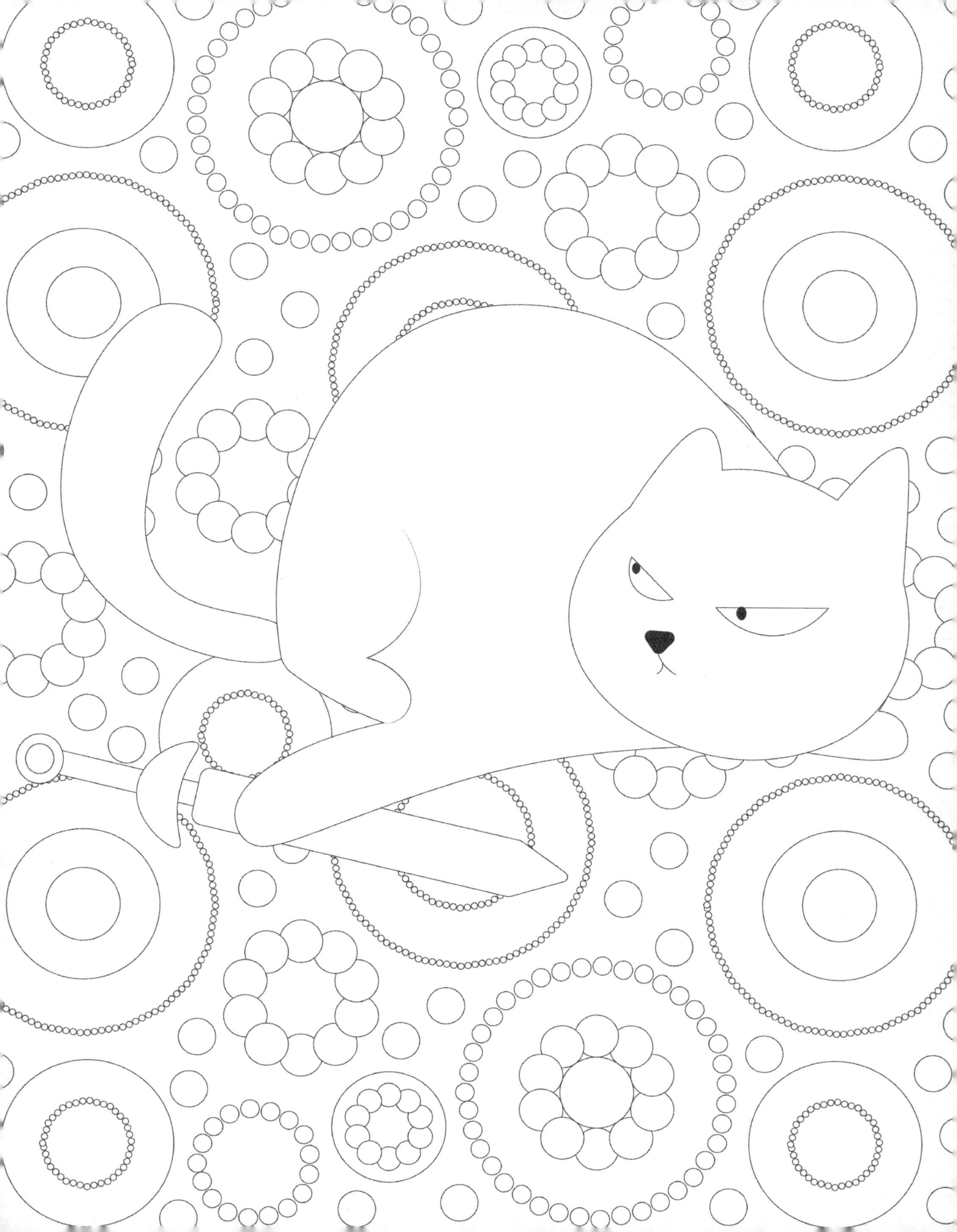

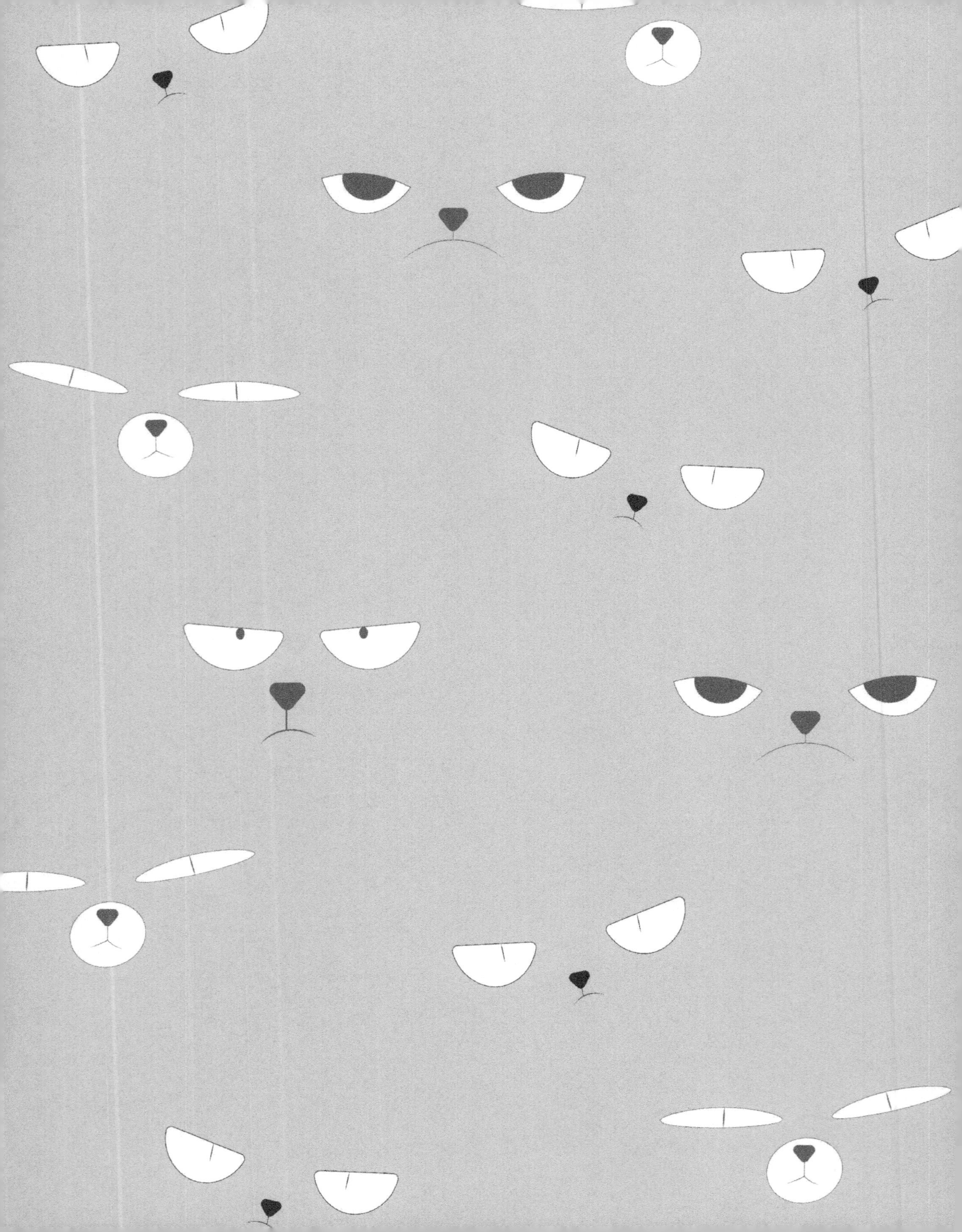

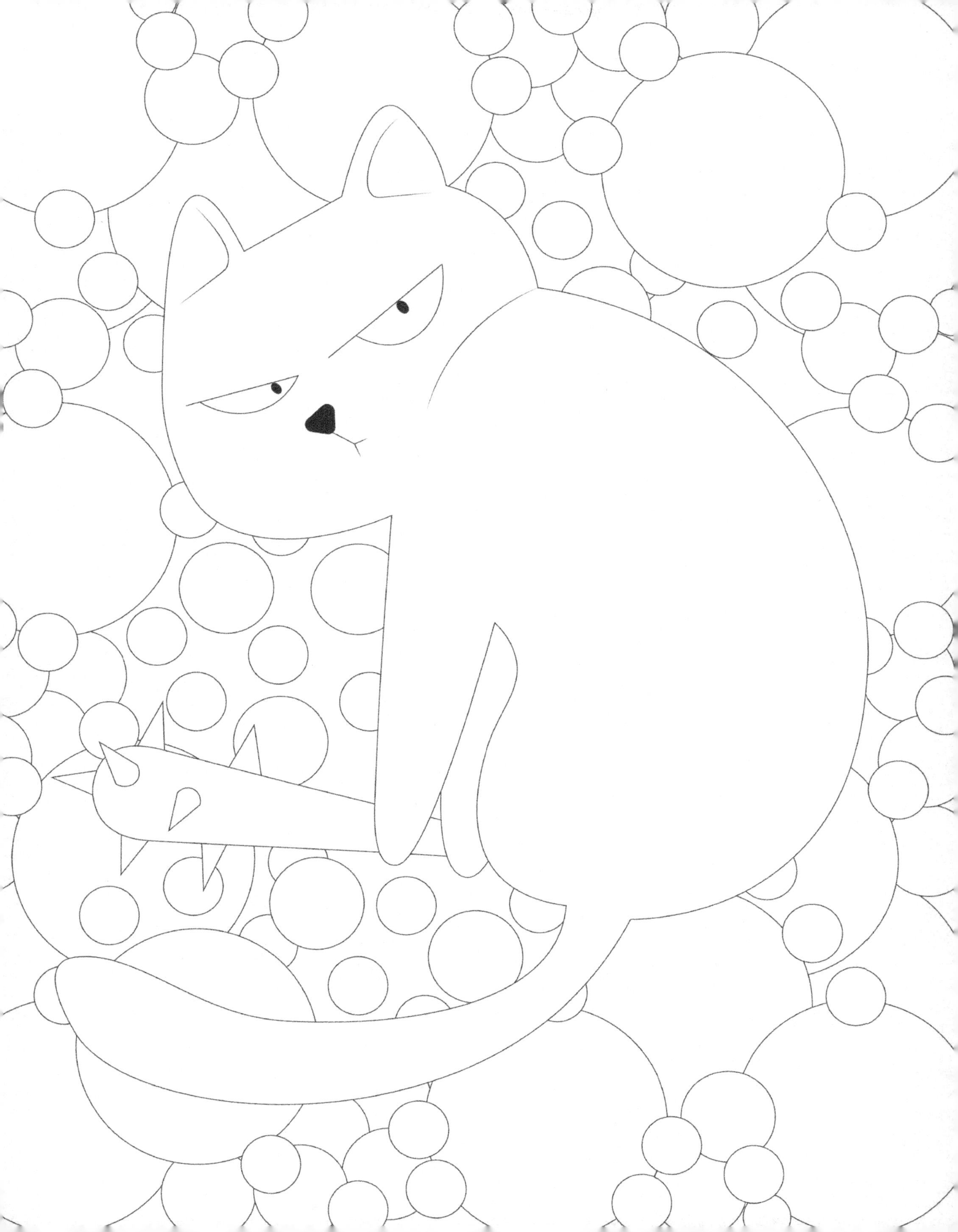

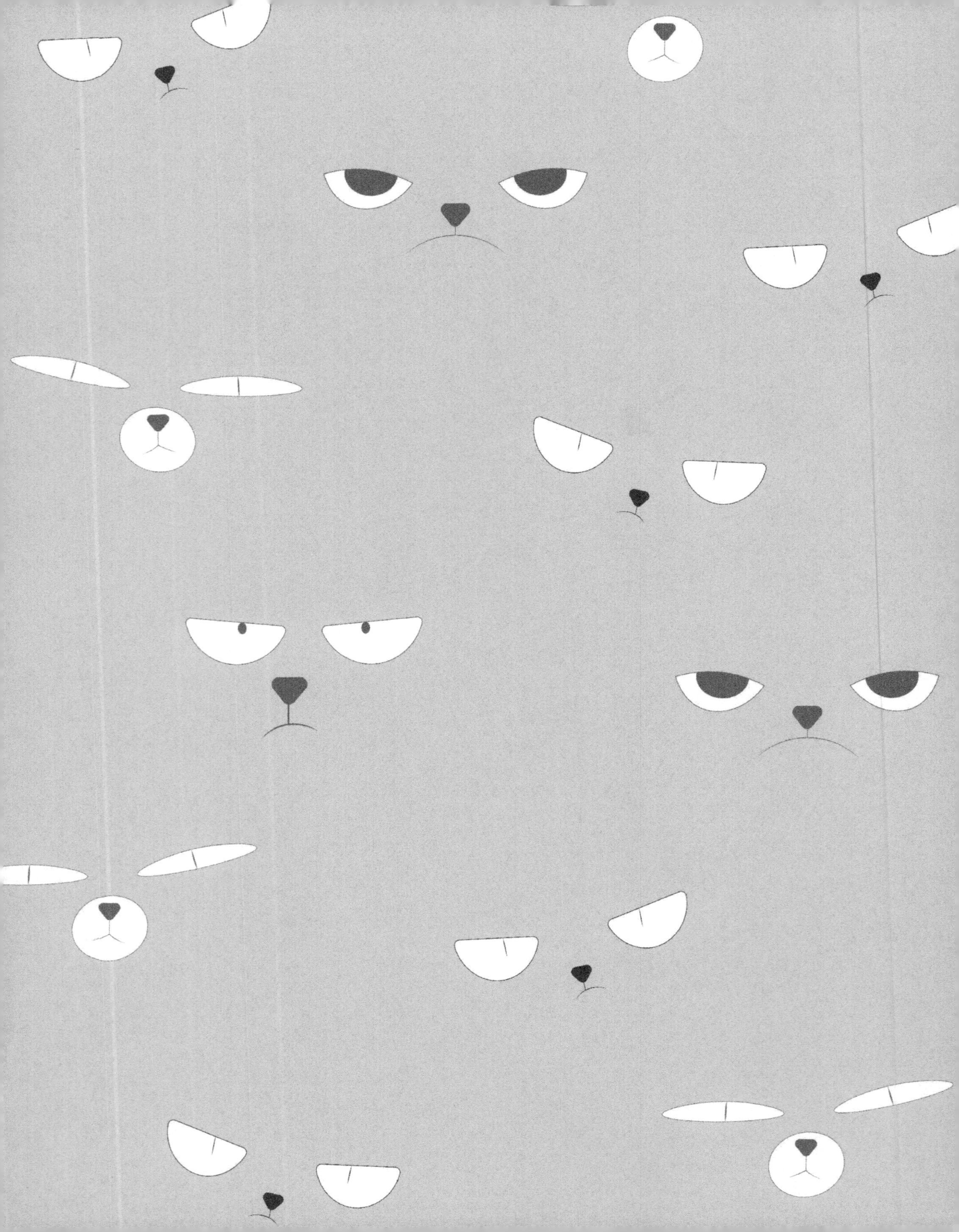

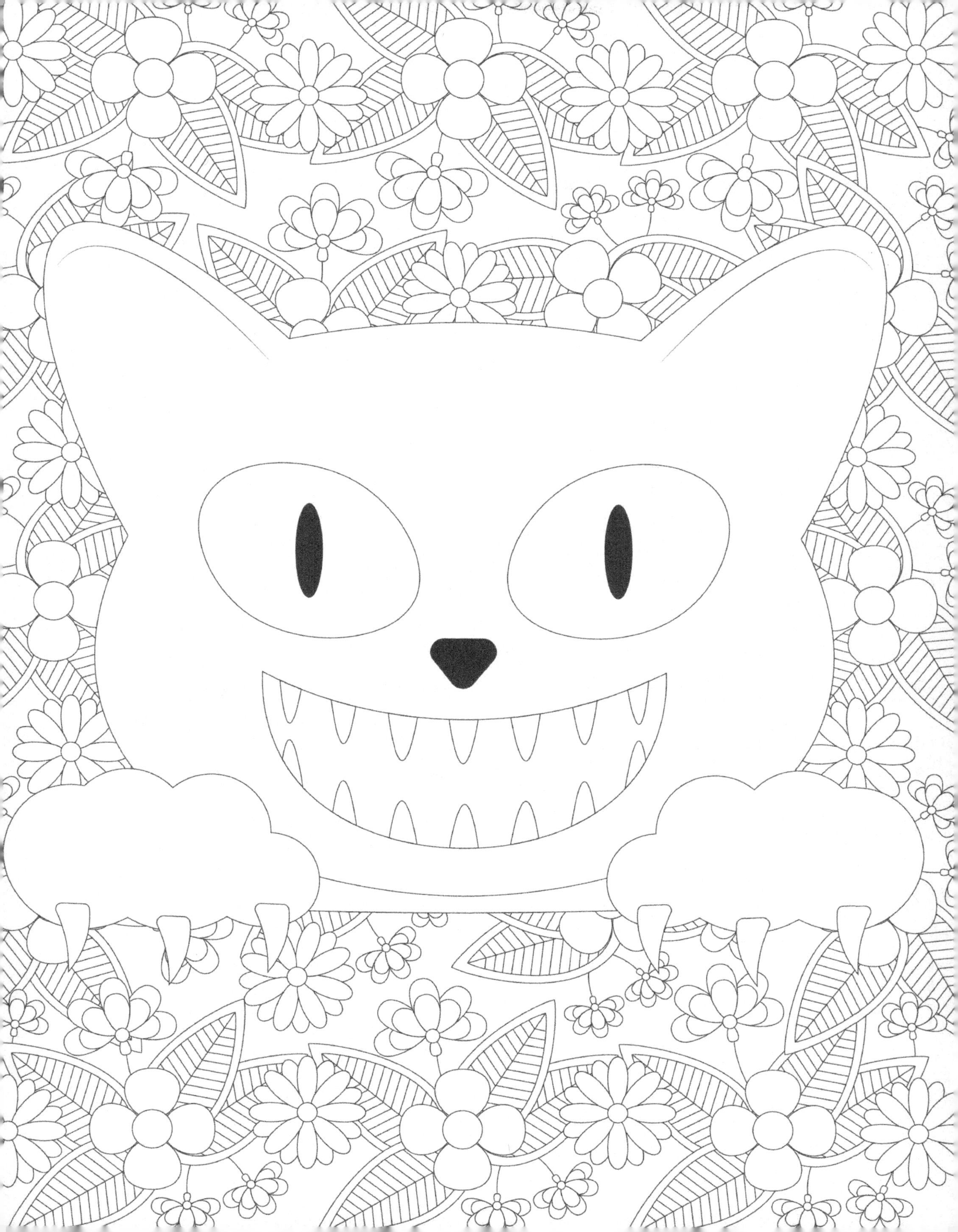

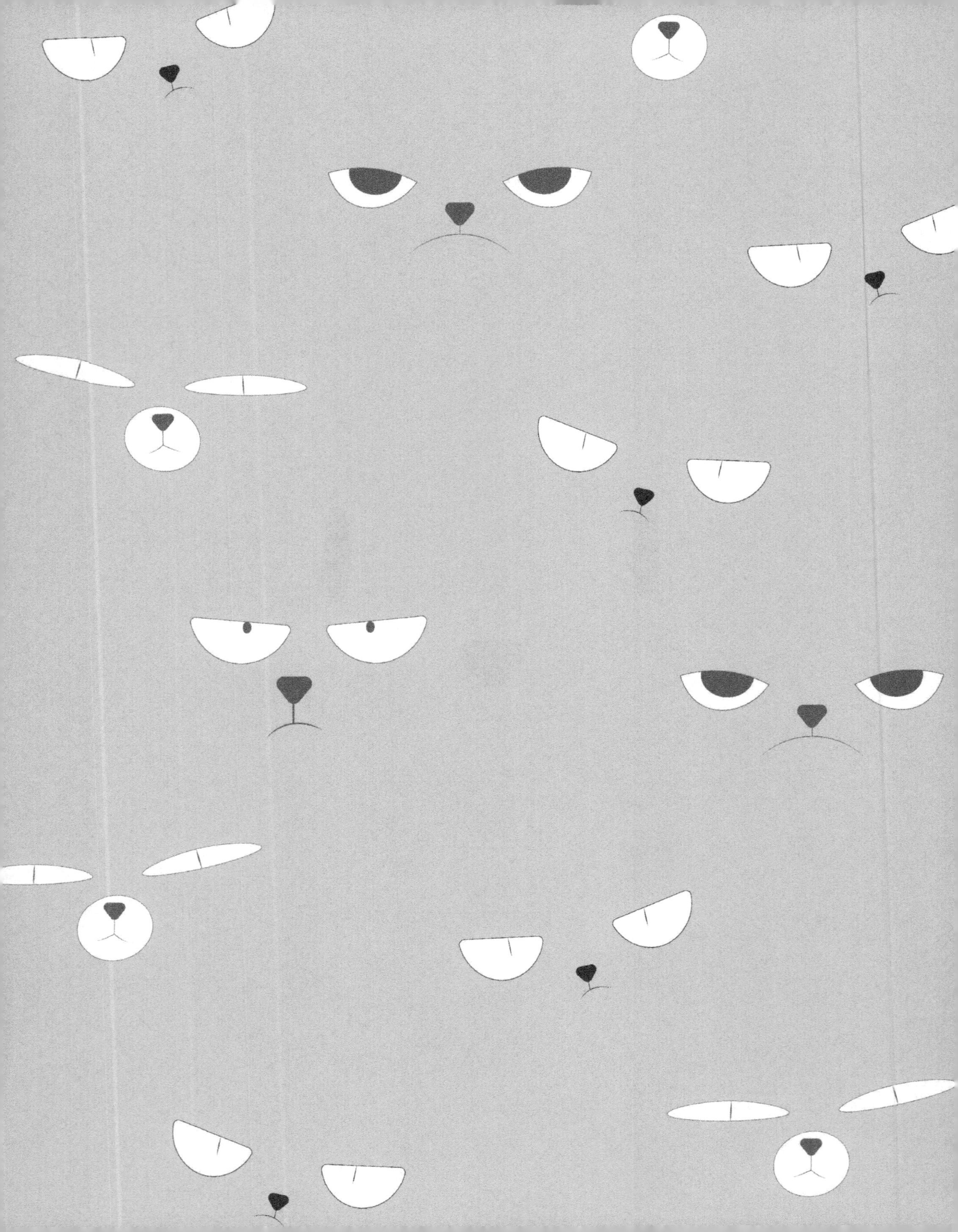

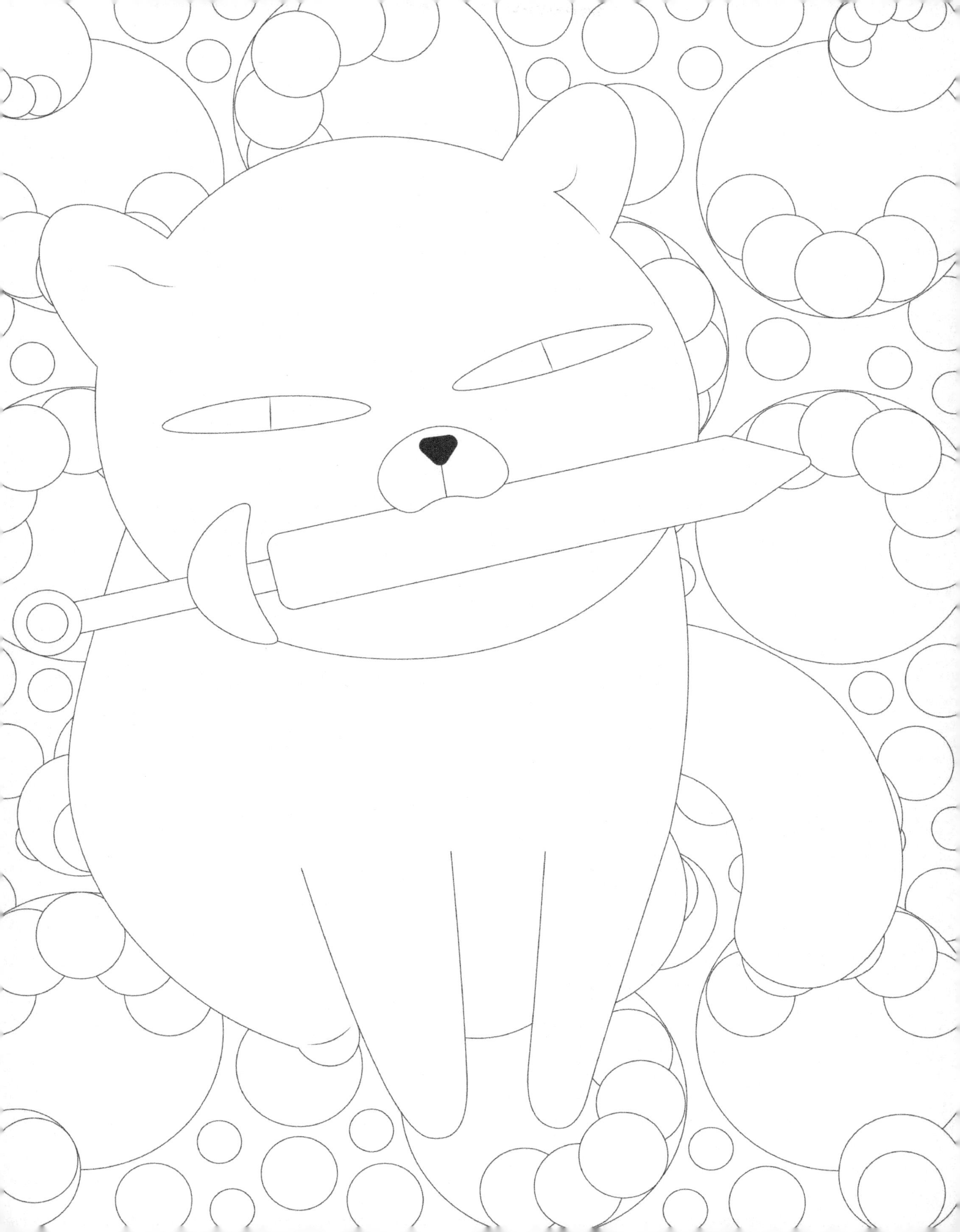

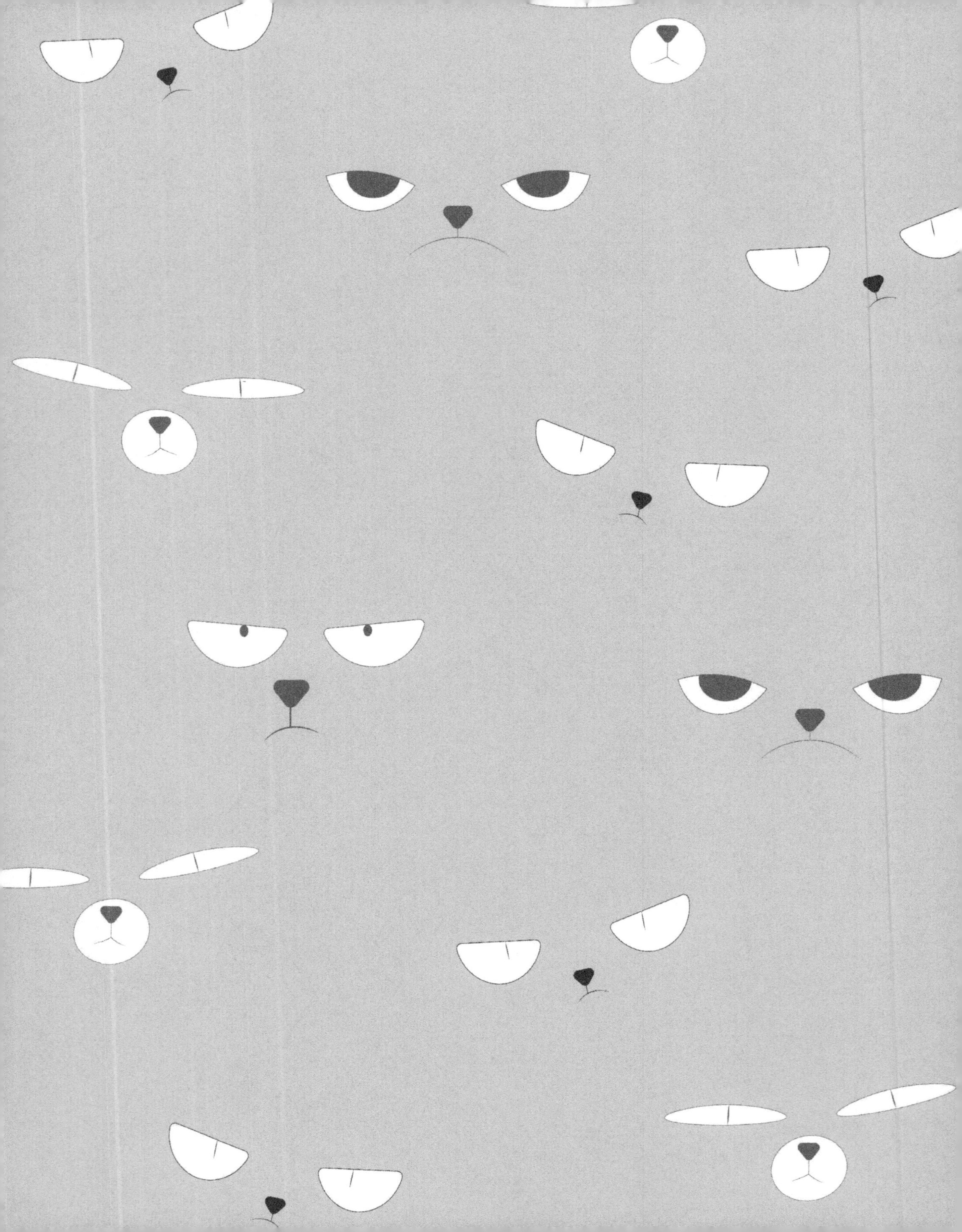

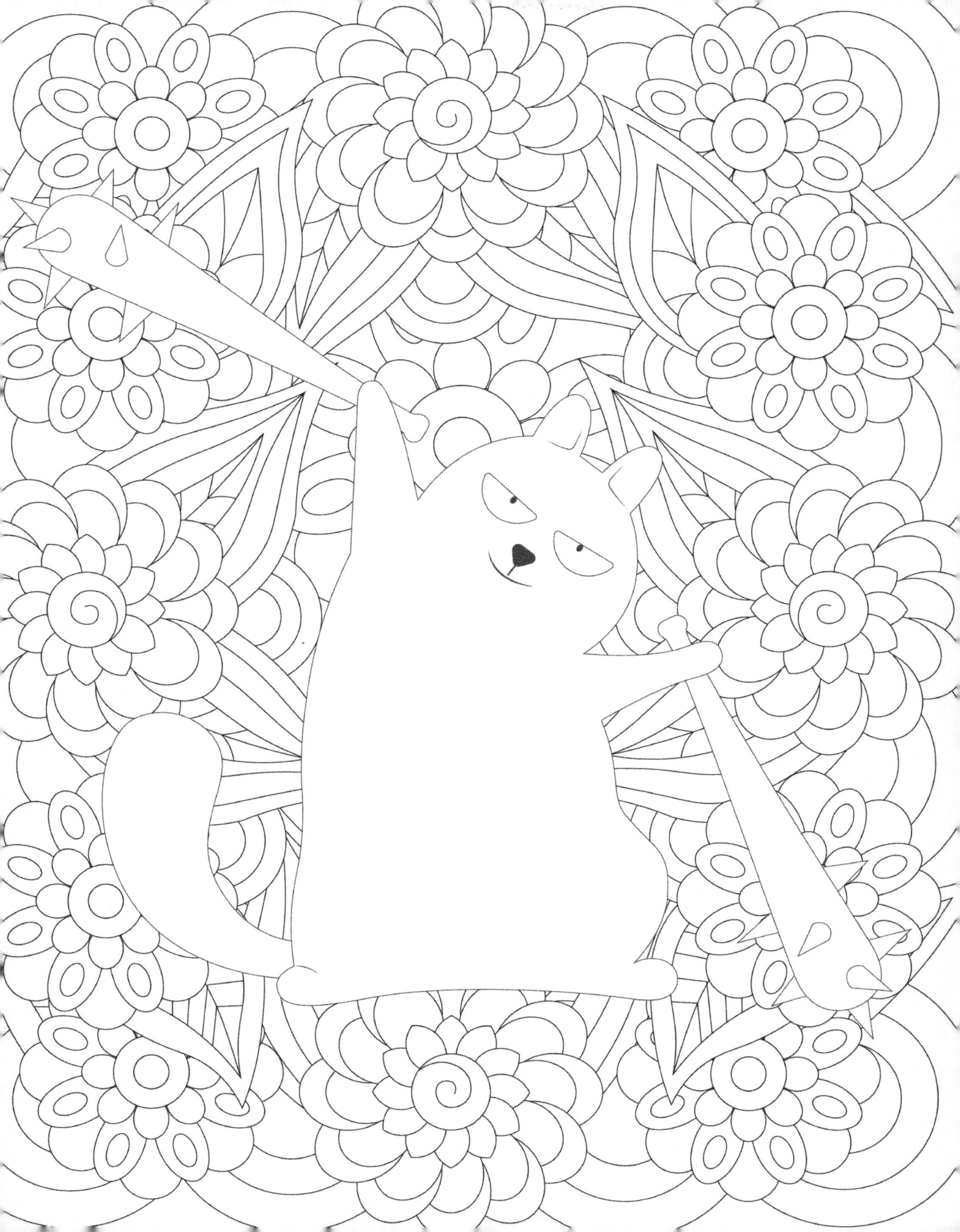

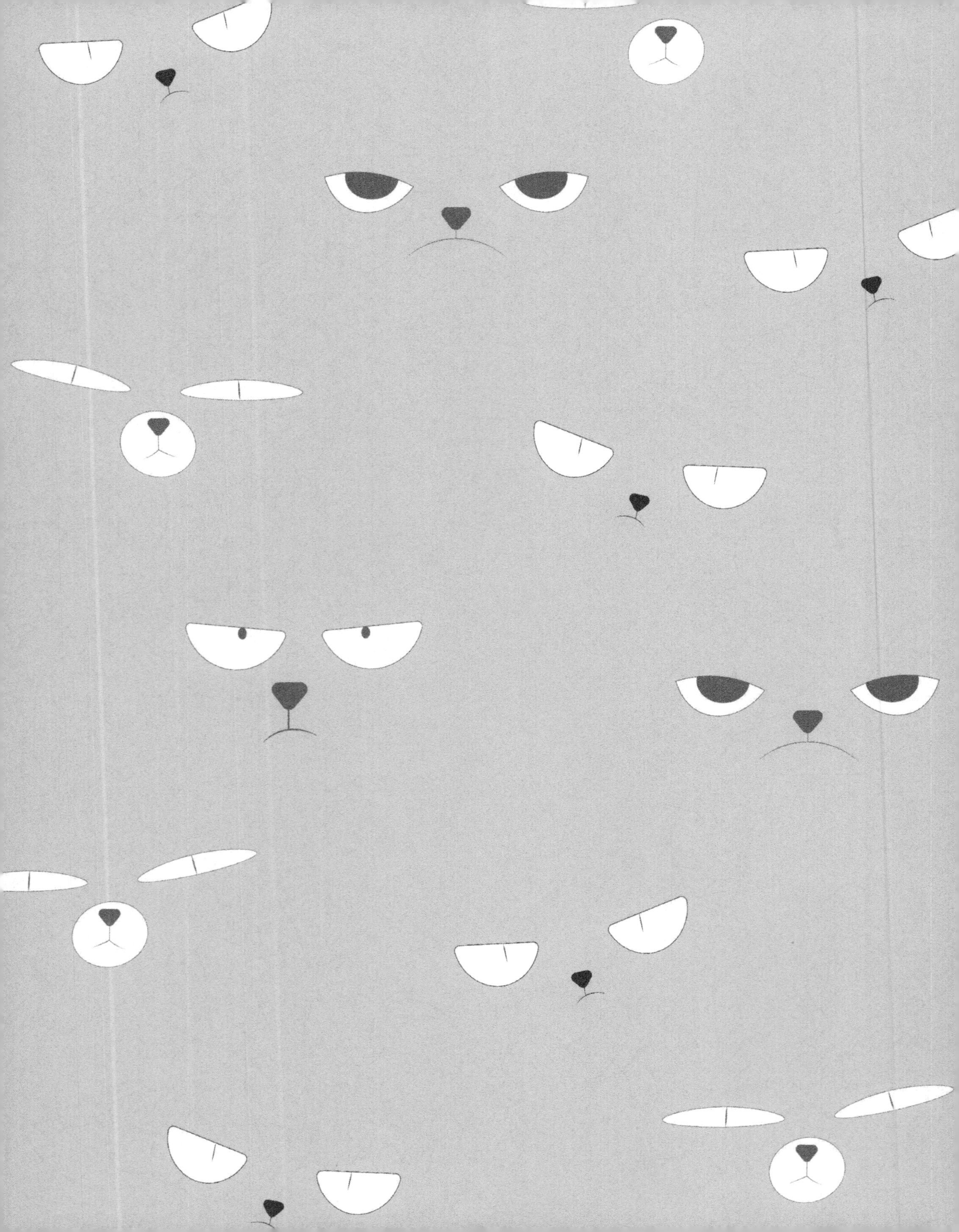

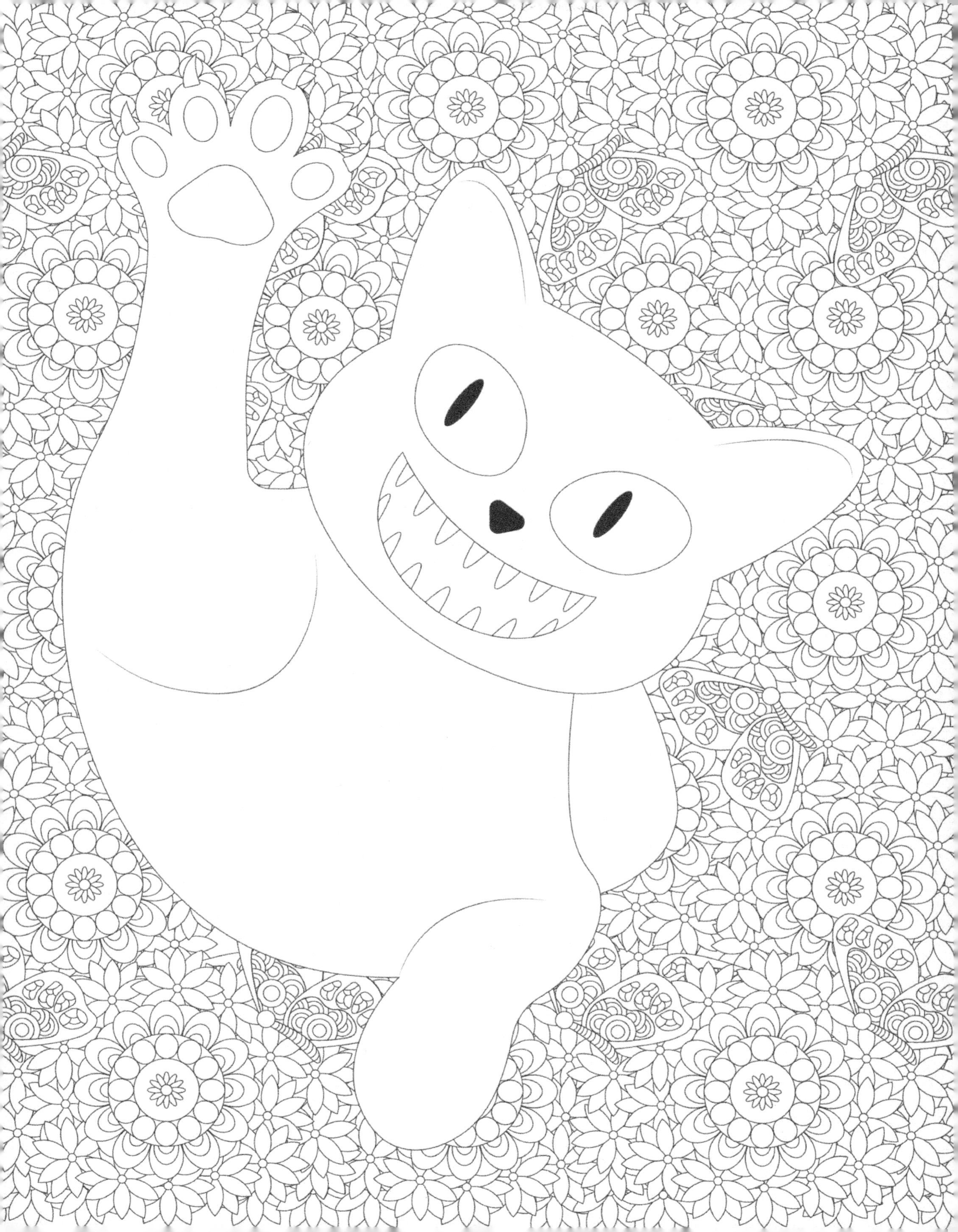

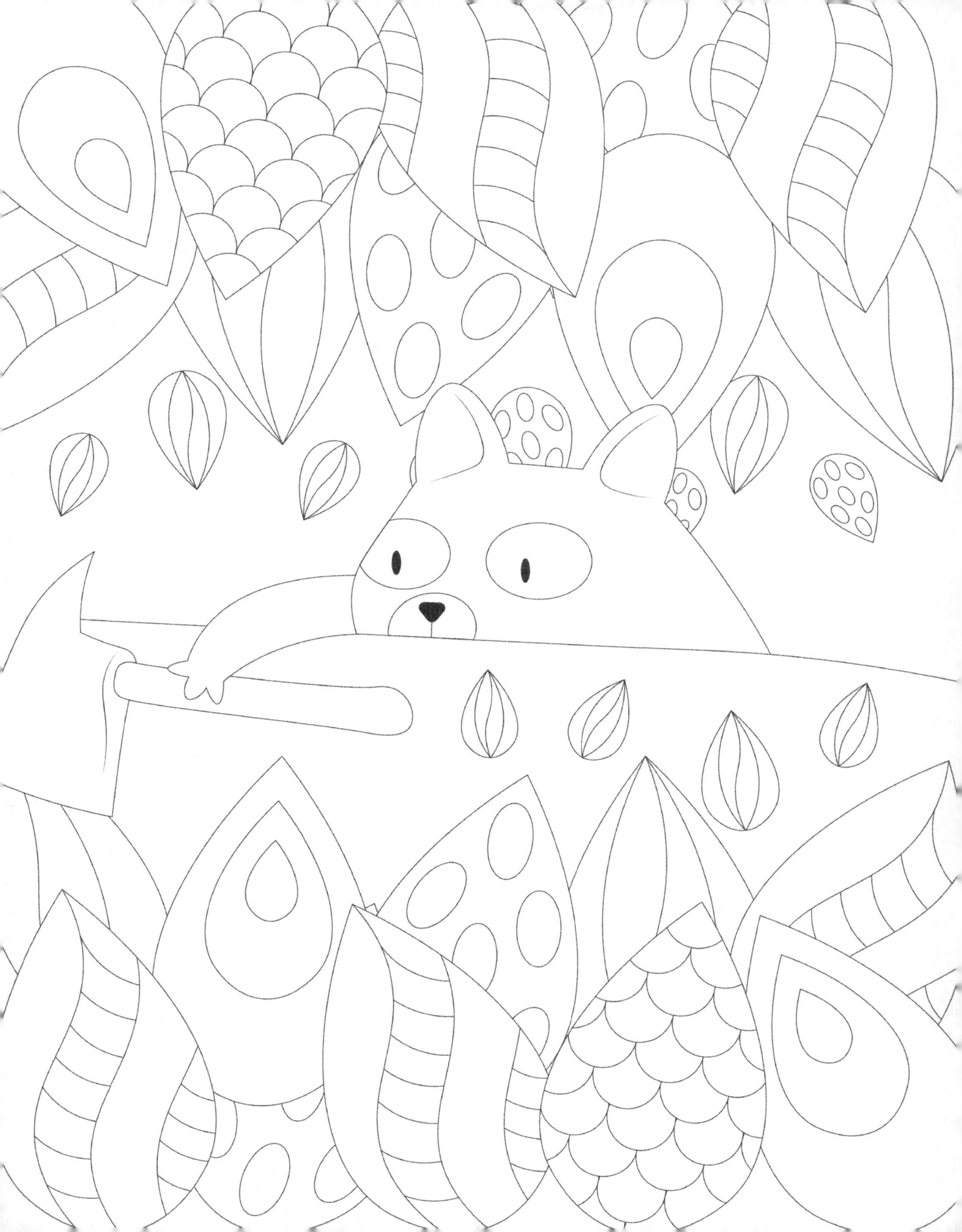

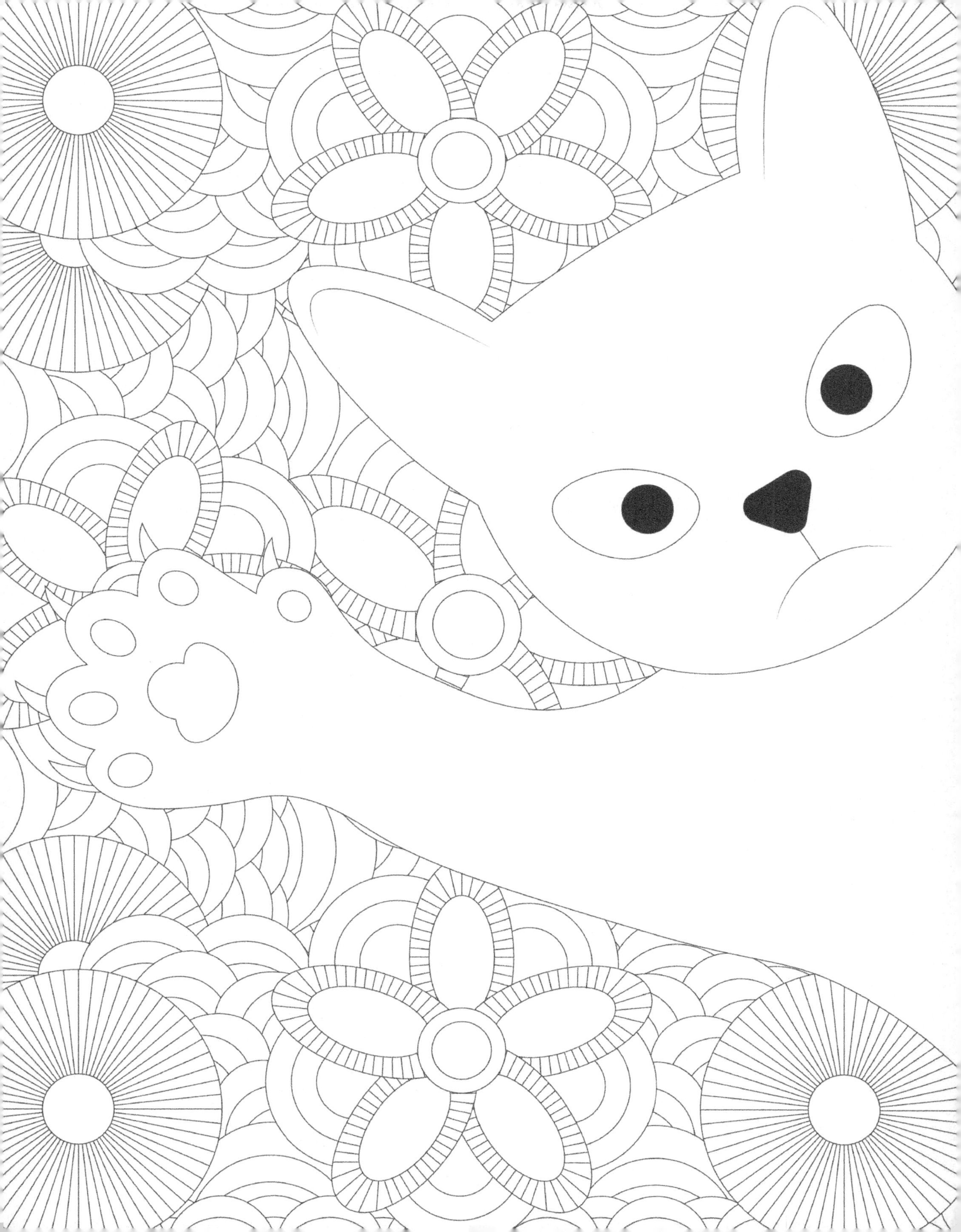

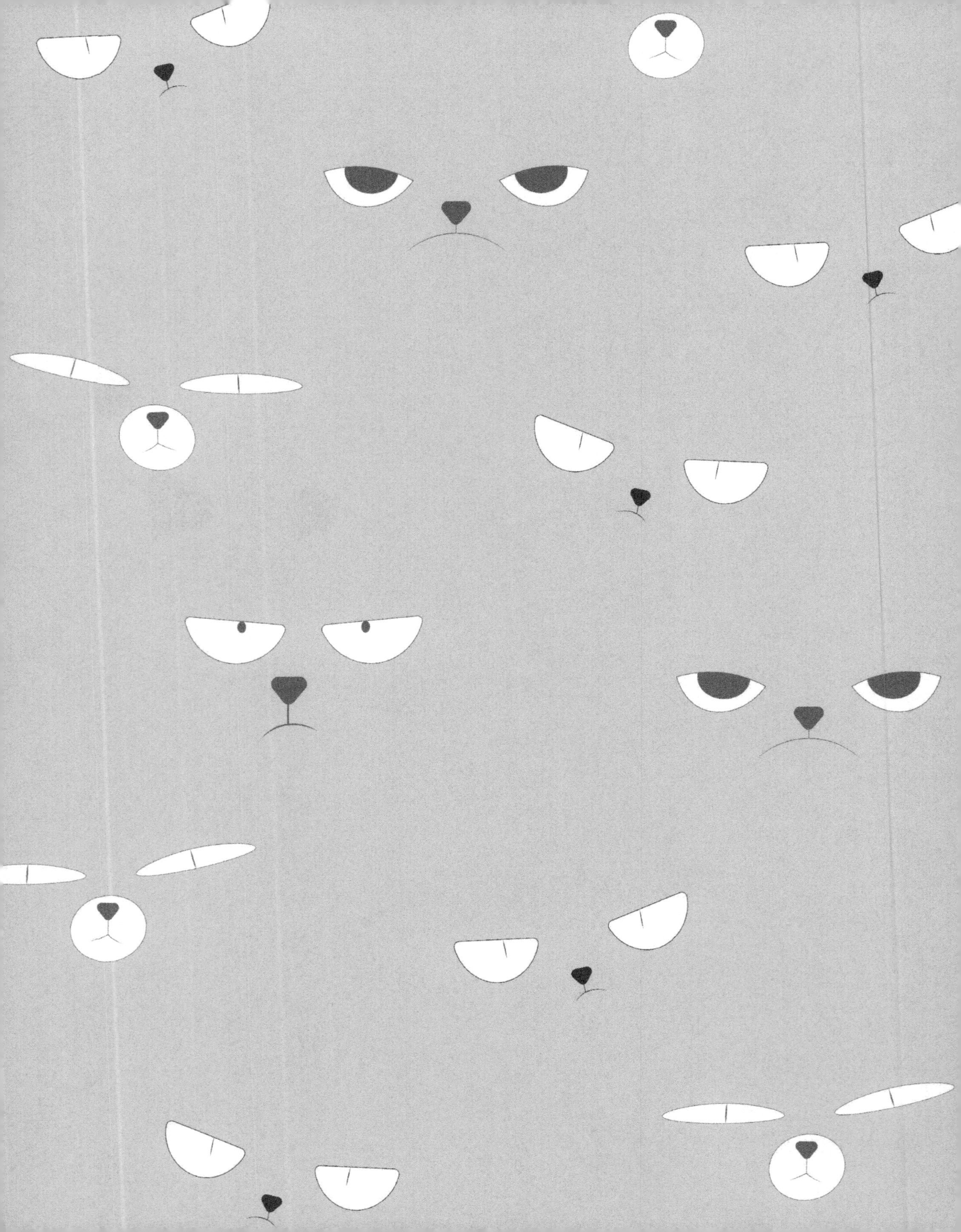

Made in the USA
Middletown, DE
26 April 2020

90635105R00038